Guiding Those Left Behind
In Minnesota

LEGAL AND PRACTICAL THINGS
YOU NEED TO DO
TO SETTLE AN ESTATE IN MINNESOTA

and

HOW TO ARRANGE YOUR OWN AFFAIRS
TO AVOID UNNECESSARY COSTS
TO YOUR FAMILY

By AMELIA E. POHL, ESQ.
with Minnesota attorney
ROLF T. NELSON, CELA

 EAGLE PUBLISHING COMPANY OF BOCA

The purpose of this book is to provide the reader with an informative overview of the subject but laws change frequently and are subject to different interpretations as courts rule on the meaning or effect of a law. This book is sold with the understanding that neither the publisher nor the authors are engaging in, nor rendering legal, accounting, medical, psychiatric, financial planning or any other professional service. If you need legal, accounting, medical, psychiatric, financial planning or other expert advice, then you should seek the services of a licensed professional.

WEB SITES: Web sites appear throughout the book. These Web sites are offered for the convenience of the reader only. Publication of these Web site addresses is not an endorsement by the authors, editors or publishers of this book.

This book is intended for use by the consumer for his or her own benefit. If you use this book to counsel someone about the law or tax matters, then that may be considered to be an unauthorized and illegal practice.

EAGLE PUBLISHING COMPANY OF BOCA
4199 N. Dixie Highway, #2
Boca Raton, FL   33431
E-mail   info@eaglepublishing.com

Printed in the United States of America
ISBN 1-892407-56-6
Library of Congress Catalog Card Number 2002100523

Amelia E. Pohl, Esq.

Before becoming an attorney in 1985, AMELIA E. POHL taught mathematics on both the high school and college level. During her tenure as Associate Professor of Mathematics at Prince George's Community College in Maryland, she wrote several books including Probability: A Set Theory Approach, Principals of Counting and Common Stock Sense.

During her practice of law Attorney Pohl observed that many people want to reduce the high cost of legal fees by performing or assisting with their own legal transactions. Attorney Pohl found that, with a bit of guidance, people are able to perform many legal transactions for themselves. Attorney Pohl utilizes her background as teacher, author and attorney to provide that "bit of guidance" to the general public in the form of self-help legal books that she has written. Amelia E. Pohl is currently "translating" this book for the remaining 49 states:

Guiding Those Left Behind In Maine,
Guiding Those Left Behind In West Virginia, etc.

Rolf T. Nelson, JD, CELA

Minnesota Consulting Attorney

ROLF T. NELSON received his B.A. and J.D. degrees from the University of Minnesota. Mr. Nelson served for ten consecutive years in the Minnesota Legislature (House and Senate) during the 1960s and 70s.

He became Minnesota's first nationally Certified Elder Law Attorney (CELA) in 1996. He earned the CELA designation from the National Elder Law Foundation (NELF), the nation's only Elder Law specialty certifying agency approved by both the American Bar Association and the Minnesota Board of Certification. His national certification was re-issued for another 5 years in 2001.

Mr. Nelson has served on NELF's national Exam Committee since 1997. He and 3 or 4 other CELA lawyers assemble and later grade the national exam offered twice each year to Elder Law attorneys across America seeking Elder Law specialty certification.

ROLF T. NELSON has practiced for more than 30 years. He founded the Estate Crafters® law firm where he currently practices in the Minneapolis suburb of Brooklyn Center, Minnesota. He and his firm practice primarily in the areas of Asset Protection, Elder Law, Estate & Tax Planning, as well as Probate and Trust Law. Mr. Nelson represents clients from all over Minnesota as well as the United States who have parents or loved ones who live in Minnesota.

In 1984, Rolf Nelson pioneered the use of the irrevocable trust, the Seniors Trust®, which protects estates from being consumed by nursing home expenses. In 1996 he developed the Seniors Family Annuity™ which also protects estates from being consumed by nursing home expenses.

Mr. Nelson is a frequent lecturer before professional and civic groups in the areas of asset protection, elder law, estate, tax and financial planning. In 1997 and 1998, Mr. Nelson was heard on KLBB Radio (1440 & 1400 AM) every Friday between 12:30 & 1:00 p.m. answering questions on his "One Minute Estate Planner" program.

Mr. Nelson is a member of the American Bar Association, the Minnesota State Bar's Sections on Elder Law and Probate & Trust and the Hennepin County Bar's Probate Committee. He is a member of the National Association of Elder Law Attorneys.

For more information Mr. Nelson can be reached by telephone at **(763) 560-4000** or by E-Mail at
rnelson@estatecrafters.com

You can visit his firm's web site at
http://www.estatecrafters.com

ACKNOWLEDGMENT

When someone dies, the family attorney is often among the first to be called. Family members have questions about whether probate is necessary, who to notify, how to get possession of the assets, etc. Over the years, as we practiced in the field of Elder Law, we noticed that the questions raised were much the same family to family. We both agreed that a book answering such questions would be of service to the general public.

We also observed, that those who had experience in settling the estate of a loved one were more understanding of the process, and better able to make decisions about their own estate plan, so we decided to combine the two topics: Settling An Estate and Estate Planning into a single book *Guiding Those Left Behind*.

The "Guiding" refers to the guidance that this book gives in the event that you need to settle the estate of your loved one. It also refers to the guidance that you can give to your loved ones by setting up your own Estate Plan so that your family is not burdened by unnecessary costs and delays in settling your estate.

We wish to thank all of the clients, whom we have had the honor and pleasure to serve, for providing us with the impetus to produce this book.

The Organization of the Book

To GUIDE THOSE LEFT BEHIND, you need to know what is involved in settling an Estate in Minnesota. This book explains the things that need to be done:

1. How to tend to the funeral and burial
2. What agencies need to be notified of the death
3. How to locate the decedent's property
4. What bills need (and do not need) to be paid
5. How to determine who is entitled to inherit the decedent's property
6. How to transfer the decedent's property to the proper beneficiary

We devoted a chapter to each of these 6 steps; and for those who are in the process of settling an Estate, we placed a CHECK LIST at the end of Chapter 6 summarizing the many things that need to be done.

Once you read Chapters 1 through 6 you will be able to identify those problems that can happen when someone dies. Using those Chapters as a base, you can set up your own Estate Plan so that your family is not burdened by similar problems. Chapter 7 Everyman's Estate Plan, suggests different methods you can use to accomplish this goal.

GLOSSARY

This book is designed for the average reader. Legal terminology has been kept to a minimum. There is a glossary at the end of the book in the event you come across a legal term that is not familiar to you.

FICTITIOUS NAMES AND EVENTS

The examples in this book are based loosely on actual events; however, all names are fictitious; and the events, as portrayed, are fictitious.

Guiding Those Left Behind
In Minnesota

CONTENTS

About The Book

We tried to make this book as comprehensive as possible so there are specialized sections of the book that do not apply to the general population and may not be of interest to you. The following GUIDE POSTS appear throughout the book. You can read the section if the situation applies to you or skip the section if it doesn't.

GUIDE POSTS

The SPOUSE POST means that the information provided is specifically for the spouse of the decedent. If the decedent was single, then skip this section.

The CALL-A-LAWYER POST alerts you to a situation that may require the assistance of an attorney. See page xiii for information about how to find a lawyer.

The CAUTION POST alerts you to a potential problem. It is followed by a suggestion about how to avoid the problem.

The SPECIAL SITUATION POST means that the information given in that paragraph applies to a particular event or situation; for example when the decedent dies a violent death. If the situation does not apply in your case then you can skip the section.

Reading the Law

Where applicable, we identified the state statute or federal statute that is the basis of the discussion. We did this as a reference, and also to encourage the general public to read the law as it is written. Prior to the Internet the only way you could look up the law was to physically take yourself to the local courthouse law library or the law section of a public library. Today all of the state and federal statutes are literally at your finger tips. They are just a mouse click away on the Internet. To look up the law all you need is the address of the Web site and the identifying number of the statute:

FEDERAL STATUTE WEB SITE
http://www4.law.cornell.edu/uscode

MINNESOTA STATUTE WEB SITE
http://www.leg.state.mn.us

The Minnesota legislature has organized their statutes into some 648 numbered Titles. For example, Title 55 is Safe Deposit Companies; Title 525 is Probate Proceeding, etc. Many of the Titles have lettered sections in addition to the numbered section, for example there is Title 49 and Title 49A.

Each Title is divided into sections. We will refer to a statute by the number of the Title and the section within that Title, for example (MN 149A.74) refers to Title 149A, section 74 of the Minnesota statutes. To look up this statute up you would go to the above Web site and type in the number of the statute in the search box.

If you come across a topic in the book that is important to you, then you may find it both interesting and profitable to read the law as it is actually written.

When You Need A Lawyer

The purpose of the book is to give the reader a basic understanding of what needs to be done when someone dies, and to provide information about how a person can arrange his own affairs to avoid problems for his own family. It is not intended as a substitute for legal counsel or any other kind of professional advice. If you have any legal question, then you should to seek the counsel of an attorney. When looking for an attorney, consider three things: EXPERTISE, COST and PERSONALITY.

EXPERTISE

The Minnesota State Bar Association currently has certification programs in the areas of Real Property and Civil Trial. The state also recognizes attorneys who have been certified by the following organizations:
Elder Law by the National Elder Law Foundation
Criminal Law by the National Board of Trial Advocacy
Family Law by the National Board of Trial Advocacy
Consumer Bankruptcy by the American Board of Certification
Business Bankruptcy by the American Board of Certification

To be certified in any of these areas, an attorney must demonstrate a high level of experience and proficiency in the field. Once certified, the attorney must fulfill ongoing educational requirements to stay current with the law.

Certification is just one of the criteria to consider. Many fine attorneys are experienced in an area of law, but have not taken the time, effort and expense to become certified as a specialist in that area of law. If the attorney is not certified in the type of law that you seek, then ask how long he has practiced that type of law and what percentage of his practice is devoted to that branch of law.

You can call the Minnesota State Bar Association at (800) 292-4152, and they will refer you to an attorney who is experienced in the type of law that you seek for an initial consultation fee of $25 for the first half hour.

Of course, the most reliable ways to find an attorney is through personal referral. Ask your friends, family or business acquaintances if they used an attorney for the field of law that you seek and whether they were pleased with the results. It is important to employ an attorney who is experienced in the area of law you seek. Your friend may have a wonderful Estate Planning attorney, but if you suffered an injury to your body, then you need an attorney who is experienced in Personal Injury.

COST

In addition to the attorney's experience, it is important to check what it will cost in attorney's fees. When you call for an appointment ask for the approximate cost for the service you seek. Also ask whether you can expect additional costs such as filing fees, accounting fees, expert witness fees, etc. If the least expensive attorney is out of your price range then you may qualify for legal assistance. You can call the Minnesota State Bar for the telephone number of the legal assistance office nearest you at (800) 292-4152, or you can visit the Minnesota Legal Services Coalition Web site for a list of programs that are currently available.

 MINNESOTA LEGAL SERVICES COALITION
http://www.mnlegalservics.org

The American Bar Association also has a directory of local Pro Bono Programs at its Web site:

 AMERICAN BAR ASSOCIATION
http://www.abanet.org/legalservices

PERSONALITY

Of equal importance to the attorney's experience and legal fees, is your relationship with the attorney. How easy was it to reach the attorney? Did you go through layers of receptionists and legal assistants before being allowed to speak to the attorney? Did the attorney promptly return your call?

If you had difficulty reaching the attorney, you can expect similar problems should you employ that attorney.

Did the attorney treat you with respect? Did the attorney treat you paternally with a "father knows best" attitude or did the attorney treat you as an intelligent person with the ability to understand the options available to you and the ability to make your own decision based on the information provided to you. Are you able to understand and easily communicate with the attorney? Is he/she speaking to you in plain English or is his/her explanation of the matter so full of legalese to be almost meaningless to you?

Do you find the attorney's personality to be pleasant or grating? Sometimes people rub each other the wrong way. It is like rubbing a cat the wrong way. Stroking a cat from head to tail is pleasing to the cat, but petting it in the opposite direction, no matter how well intended, causes friction. If the lawyer makes you feel annoyed or uncomfortable, then find another attorney.

It is worth the effort to take the time to interview as many attorneys as it takes to find one with the right expertise, fee schedule and personality for you.

The First Week 1

Dealing with the death of a close family member or friend is difficult. Not only do you need to deal with your own emotions, but often with those of your family and friends. Sometimes their sorrow is more painful to you, than what you are experiencing yourself.

In addition to the emotional impact of a death, there are many things that need to be done, from arranging the funeral and burial, to closing out the business affairs of the *decedent* (the person who died) and finally giving whatever property is left to the proper beneficiary.

The funeral and burial take only a few days. Wrapping up the affairs of the decedent may take considerably longer. This chapter explains what things you (the spouse or closest family member) need to do during the first week, beginning at the moment of death and continuing through the funeral.

 MALE GENDER USED

Rather than use "he/she" or "his/her" for simplicity
(and hoping not to offend anyone)
we will refer to the decedent and his
Personal Representative using the male gender.

References to other people will be in both genders.

THE AUTOPSY

In today's high tech world of medicine, doctors are fairly certain of the cause of death, but if there is a question as to the cause of death, the doctor may ask the person who is taking responsibility for the burial, to consent to the proceeding. Minnesota law gives an order of priority for who has the right to control the disposition of the body:

  1st   the person appointed in a Health Care Directive signed by the decedent prior to his death.
  2nd   the surviving spouse
  3rd   the decedent's child, or a majority of his children
  4th   the surviving parent or parents
  5th   the decedent's sibling or a majority of his siblings
  6th   the next of kin
  7th   the appropriate public or Court authority

(MN149A.80).

Whoever authorizes the procedure must agree to pay for the autopsy because the cost is not covered under most health insurance plans. And that cost can be significant; running anywhere from several hundred dollars to well over three thousand dollars. But it is in the family's best interest to consent to the autopsy. The examination might reveal a genetic disorder, that could be treated if it later appears in another family member. Death from a car "accident" may have been a heart attack at the wheel. Perhaps the patient who died suddenly in a hospital was misdiagnosed. The nursing home resident could have died from negligence and not old age. Even if none of these are found, knowing the cause of death with certainty is better than not knowing.

That was the case with the family of a woman who was taken to the hospital complaining of stomach pains. The doctors thought she might be suffering from gallbladder disease but she died before they could effectively treat her. A doctor suggested that an autopsy be performed to determine the actual cause of death. The woman had three daughters, one of whom objected to the autopsy: "Why spend that kind of money? It won't bring Mom back."

The daughter's wishes were respected, however over the years as they aged and became ill with their own various ailments they would undergo physical examinations. As part of taking their medical history, doctors routinely asked "And what was the cause of your mother's death?"

None could answer the question.

This is not a dramatic story. No mysterious genetic disorder ever occurred in any of her daughters, nor in any of their children. But each daughter (including the one who objected) at some point in her life, was confronted with the nagging question "What did Mom die of?"

MANDATORY AUTOPSIES

AUTOPSIES PERFORMED BY CORONER
When a person dies, a physician must sign a medical certification stating the cause of death. This is not a problem if a person dies in a hospital or nursing home from natural causes. But if a person dies suddenly at home, for whatever reason, whoever discovers the body must call 911 to summon the police. If the death was expected, the treating physician can be contacted to sign the medical certificate verifying that the decedent died of natural causes. If the decedent was not under the care of a physician, the police will call the Coroner to determine the cause of death.

The Coroner or Medical Examiner will order an autopsy in all of the following circumstances:

⇨ any violent death whether a homicide, suicide or accident;

⇨ death of an inmate of a public institutions who was not hospitalized for any organic disease;

⇨ a death caused by fire;

⇨ a death in which there are unexplained, unusual or mysterious circumstances (MN 390.32).

Autopsies ordered by the Coroner are paid for by the County (MN 357.11)

Once the Coroner takes possession of a body, it will not be released until the examination is complete. In the interim, the family can proceed with arrangements for the funeral. The funeral director will contact the Coroner to determine when he can pick up the body and proceed with the funeral arrangements.

AUTOPSIES PERFORMED BY THE INSURANCE COMPANY

Under Minnesota law, companies that issue accident and health insurance policies are required to include a provision in their contract that the company has the right to perform an autopsy (MN 62A.04). The cost of the autopsy is paid for by the insurance company, so they will not order an autopsy unless there is some important reason to do so.

ANATOMICAL GIFTS

Hospital personnel determine whether a mortally ill patient is a candidate for an organ donation. Early on in the donor program those over 65 were not considered as suitable candidates. Today, however, the condition of the organ, and not the age, is the determining factor.

The federal government has established regional Organ Procurement Organizations throughout the United States to coordinate the donor program. LifeSource, Upper Midwest Organ Procurement Organization, Inc. ("LifeSource") is the organization that services Minnesota. If it is decided that the patient is a candidate, the hospital will contact LifeSource. The doctor who is treating the patient together with LifeSource will determine whether the patient is a suitable donor.

GIFT AUTHORIZED PRIOR TO DEATH

If, before death, the decedent made an anatomical gift by signing a donor card as part of his driver's license, or signing a health care directive authorizing the gift, then hospital personnel or the donor's doctor need to be made aware of the gift in quick proximity to the time of death — preferably before death. If it is determined that the donation is medically acceptable, the gift will be made. No family member need give permission, provided the hospital has a copy of the decedent's unrevoked donor card (MN 171.07, 525.9211).

GIFT AUTHORIZED BY THE FAMILY

If no donor card is on record, and it is determined that the decedent is a suitable donor, someone who is specially trained will approach the family to request permission for the donation.

Minnesota statute states an order of priority for those who can give permission for an anatomical gift:

1st spouse   2nd adult son or daughter
3rd either parent   4th adult brother or sister
5th a grandparent
6th the guardian or conservator of the decedent at time of death or a Health Care Agent or Proxy appointed by the decedent prior to his death.

Every effort must be made to contact those people with highest priority. No gift can be made if someone with the same or a higher priority objects. For example, if the sister of the decedent agrees to the gift (4th in priority) and the decedent had an adult child (2nd in priority), the child needs to be made aware of the gift. If the child objects, no gift can be made. Similarly, the statute prohibits the gift if the decedent refused to make an anatomical gift during his lifetime and did not change his mind prior to death (MN 5525.9211, 525.9212).

AFTER THE DONATION

Once the donation is made the body is delivered to the funeral home and prepared for burial or cremation as directed by the family. The donation does not disfigure the body so there can be an open casket viewing if the family so wishes.

Some regional Organ Procurement Organizations have an aftercare program that includes a letter of condolence to the family and an expression of gratitude for the gift. For privacy reasons, the identity of the recipient of the gift is not disclosed, but on request from the family, the local Organ Procurement Organization will give the family basic demographic information about the donation, such as the age, sex, marital status, number of children and occupation of the recipient of the gift.

GIFT FOR EDUCATION OR RESEARCH

If the decedent signed a donor card indicating his wish to use his body for any purpose and he is not a candidate for an organ donation, then you can offer to release the body for the purpose of education or research. There are two facilities located in Minnesota:

Department of Anatomy Bequest Program   (612) 625-1111
2-155 Jackson Hall
University of Minnesota
321 Church Street
Minneapolis, MN   55455

Mayo Clinic, Section of Anatomy   (507) 284-2693
Medical Science Building 3
200 First Street, S.W.
Rochester, MN 55905

The study can take up to 18 months to complete. At the end of the study the remains can be returned to the family, however, most families opt for cremation. There is no charge to the family for local transportation to the facility, nor for the cremation once the study is complete. If the family wants the body returned, then the cost of the final disposition is paid for by the family.

If the family authorizes a cremation, then the *cremains* (cremated remains) will be placed in a communal scatter garden that is local to the facility; or if the family wishes, the cremains will be delivered to the next of kin.

CAVEAT: Federal law prohibits payment for organ donations (42 U.S.C. 274 e). There is no ban on payments made to prepare organs or tissue for transplantation, nor is there any ban on charges made to transport bodies or body parts. Not-for profit and as well as for-profit companies have sprung up that are in the business of preparing and delivering body parts. These companies request donations from families — so they are violating federal law by paying for the donation. The company prepares the body tissue or other parts of the donated body, and then distributes the parts throughout the United States to physicians, hospitals, research centers, etc. In many cases the monies charged for preparation and transportation includes a sizable profit. If a company or organization other than your local Organ Procurement Organization approaches you to make a donation, then before making the donation you may want to learn about the company requesting the donation.

> What is the name of the company?
> Where are their main headquarters located?
> What is their primary business activity?
> What is the name and job description of the
> person making the request?

DETERMINE THE END USE OF THE DONATION

You may want to ask what they intend to do with the tissue or body part. If it is being used for research, then what type of research? Where is the research being conducted? If it will be used for transplantation, then what agency (doctor, hospital) will receive the donation and where is that agency located?

Once you have this information you can make an informed decision as to whether you wish to make the donation.

THE FUNERAL

Approximately ten percent of deaths occur suddenly because of accident, suicide, foul play or undetected illness. But, in general, death occurs after a lengthy illness, with a common scenario being that of an aged person who dies after being ill for several months, if not years. In such case, family and friends are emotionally prepared for the happening. Expected or not, the first job is the disposition of the body.

THE PREARRANGED FUNERAL

Increasingly, people are arranging, in advance, for their own funeral and burial. This makes it easier on the family both financially and emotionally. All the decisions have been made and there is no guessing what the decedent would have wanted.

If the decedent made provision for his burial, then you should come across a burial certificate, or perhaps a deed to a burial space. If he made provision for his funeral, you should find a Preneed Funeral Agreement. If you cannot locate the Agreement, but you know the decedent made provision for his burial and funeral, call the funeral home and ask them to send you a copy of the Agreement. If you believe the decedent arranged for his funeral, but you do not know the name of the funeral home, then check with all the local funeral homes. Many funeral homes are owned by national firms with computer capacity to identify people who have purchased a Funeral Agreement in any of their many locations.

Once you have possession of the Agreement, take it with you to the funeral home and go over the terms with the funeral director. You need to determine what items are covered by the Agreement and whether you can expect any additional charge.

MAKING FUNERAL ARRANGEMENTS

If the decedent died unexpectedly or without having made any prior funeral arrangements then your first job is to choose a funeral director and make arrangements for the funeral or cremation. Most people choose the nearest or most conveniently located funeral home without comparison shopping. However prices for these services can vary significantly from funeral home to funeral home. Savings can be had if you take the time to make a few phone calls.

Receiving price quotes by telephone is your right under Federal law. Federal Trade Commission ("FTC") Rule 453.2 (b) (1) requires a funeral director to give an accurate telephone quote of the prices of his goods and services. Funeral homes are listed in the telephone directory under FUNERAL DIRECTORS. If you live in a small town, there may be only one or two listings. If such is the case, then check out some funeral homes in the next largest city.

Funeral directors usually provide the following services:
➢ arrange for the transportation of the body
   to the funeral home and then to the burial site
➢ obtain burial transit permits
➢ arrange for the embalming or cremation of the body
➢ arrange funeral and memorial services
   and the viewing of the body
➢ obtain information for the death certificate
➢ order copies of the death certificate for the family
➢ have memorial cards printed.

To compare prices you will need to determine which of the above services are included in the basic funeral plan and whether you can expect any additional cost.

It may be necessary to have the body embalmed if you are going to have a viewing; but embalming is not necessary if you order a direct cremation or an immediate burial. Federal and state law prohibit the funeral home from charging an embalming fee unless you order the service (FTC Rule 453.5; MN 149A.74).

If the decedent did not own a burial space, then that cost must be included when making funeral arrangements.

PURCHASING THE CASKET

When comparison-shopping, you will find that the single most expensive item in the funeral arrangement is the casket. Funeral directors will quote you a price for the basic funeral plan. That plan does not usually include the cost of the casket. Directors will quote a range of prices for the casket with a brief description of the type of casket.

When selecting a casket you should be aware that there is often a considerable mark-up in the price quoted by the funeral director. You do not need to go "sole source" when purchasing casket. You can purchase the casket elsewhere and have it delivered to the funeral home to be used instead of the one offered by the funeral director.

In 1994, The Federal Trade Commission ruled that funeral homes had to accept caskets purchased elsewhere. Both state and federal law prohibit the funeral home from charging a handling fee or surcharge for accepting a casket purchased elsewhere (FTC Rule 453.4)

Caskets are not usually displayed for sale in a shopping mall, so most of us have no idea of the going price for a casket. With the advent of the Internet, you can learn all about the cost of any item, even a casket, by using your search engine to find a retail casket sales dealer. If you are not computer literate, you can locate the nearest retail casket sales outlet by looking in the yellow pages under CASKETS. You may need to look in the telephone directory for the nearest large city to find a listing. By making a call to a retail casket sales dealer, you will become knowledgeable in the price range of caskets. You can then decide what is a reasonable price for the product you seek.

The best time to do your comparison shopping, is before you go to the funeral home to arrange for the funeral. Once you have determined what you should pay for the casket, it is only fair to give the funeral director the opportunity to meet that price. If you cannot reach a meeting of the minds, then you can always order the casket from the retail sales dealer and have it delivered to the funeral home.

ON-LINE FUNERAL SERVICES

The Internet is changing the way the world does business, and the funeral industry is no exception. A growing number of mortuaries are offering live Webcasts of funerals and wakes for those who are unable to pay their respects in person.

There are Web sites such as ObitDetails.com where you can post an obituary. There are on-line memorial chat rooms as well as online eulogies and testimonials. There is even a Web site that offers a posthumous e-mail service which allows people to leave final messages for friends and relatives.

THE CREMATION

Increasingly people are opting for cremation. The reasons for choosing cremation are varied, but for the majority, it is a matter of finances. The cost of cremation is approximately one-sixth that of an ordinary funeral and burial. A major saving is the cost of the casket. You will need to arrange for a suitable container to deliver the body to the crematory; however no casket is necessary for the cremation. Both federal and state law prohibit a funeral director from saying that a casket is required for a direct cremation. (MN 149A.73, FTC Rule 453.3 (b)ii).

If you are having a memorial service in a place of worship and no viewing of the body before the cremation, consider contracting with a facility that does cremations only. Look in the telephone book **CREMATION SERVICES**. You will also see cremation "societies" in the telephone book. Some are for-profit and others non-profit. You can also find advertisements for cremation services on the Internet.

THE OVERWEIGHT DECEDENT
If the decedent weighs more than 300 pounds, then you need to check to see if the cremation service has facilities large enough to handle the body. If you cannot locate a crematory that can accommodate the body, you will need to make burial arrangements.

THE DECEDENT WITH A PACEMAKER
Cremating a body with a pacemaker or any radiation producing devise can cause damage to the cremation chamber or to the person performing the cremation. The cremation cannot take place unless such device is removed (MN 149A.95). If the decedent was wearing an electronic aid, you need to ask the funeral director or cremation service director about the cost of its removal.

DISPOSING OF THE ASHES

The decedent's cremains can be placed in a cemetery. Many cemeteries have a separate building called a *columbarium*, which is especially designed to store urns. If not, then the cremains can be placed in a cemetery plot. Some cemeteries allow the cremains of a family member to be placed in an occupied family plot. Similarly, some cemeteries will allow the cremains to be placed in a space in the mausoleum that is currently occupied by a member of the decedent's family. If it is your desire to have the cremains placed in an occupied mausoleum or family plot, then you need to call the cemetery and ask them to explain their policy as it relates to the burial of urns in occupied sites.

If the cremains are to be placed in a cemetery, then you need to obtain a suitable urn for the burial. You can purchase the urn from the funeral director or cremation service director. Urns cost much less than caskets, but they can cost several hundred dollars. You may wish to do some comparison shopping by calling a retail sales casket dealer.

The decedent may have expressed a desire that his ashes be spread out to sea. The funeral director or cremation service director can assist you with such arrangements.

ABANDONED CREMAINS
It sometimes happens that the decedent is cremated and no one comes back to pick the cremains. After 30 days the cremation director will send written notice to whoever has authority to dispose of the cremains. If there is no response, after 120 days, the cremation director may dispose of the cremains in any lawful manner (MN 149A.95).

If the decedent is to be buried in another state, then the body will need to be transported to that state. Many states, including Minnesota, require a Transit Permit for burial or removal from the state where the death occurred (MN 149A.93, 149A.94). If services are to be held in Minnesota and in another state, then contact a local funeral director and he will make arrangements with the out-of-state funeral home for the transportation of the body.

If you do not plan to have services conducted in Minnesota, you can contact the out-of-state funeral director and ask him to effect the transfer. Most funeral homes belong to a national network of funeral homes, so the both local and the out-of-state funeral director usually have the means to make arrangements to transport the body.

TRANSPORTING CREMAINS

If the body has been cremated, you can transport the cremains yourself, either by carrying the ashes as part of your luggage or by arranging with the airline to transport the ashes as cargo. Have a certified copy of the death certificate and the Transit Permit ready in the event that you need to identify the cremains of the decedent.

In these days of heightened security, it is important to call the airline before departure and ask whether they have any special regulation or procedure regarding the transportation of human ashes.

SPOUSE ▷ THE MILITARY BURIAL

Subject to availability of burial spaces, an honorably discharged veteran, his dependent child and his surviving spouse may be buried in any of two military cemeteries located in Minnesota:

FORT SNELLING NATIONAL CEMETERY
7601 34th Avenue, South
Minneapolis, MN   55450-1199
Telephone: (612) 726-1127

MINNESOTA STATE VETERANS CEMETERY
15550 Highway 115
Little Falls, MN 56345
Telephone (320) 616-2527

You can call the cemetery for information about what documents are needed for the burial.

An honorably discharged veteran can also be buried in a national military cemetery. The Department of the Army is in charge of the Arlington National Cemetery. If you wish to have an eligible deceased veteran buried in the Arlington National Cemetery, then call them at (703) 695-3250 or write to them at:

Arlington National Cemetery
Interment Service Branch
Arlington, VA 22211

Special Situation	THE COST OF A MILITARY BURIAL

Burial space in a National Cemetery is free of charge. Cemetery employees will open and close the grave and mark it with headstone or grave marker without cost to the family. The local Veteran's Administration ("VA") will provide the family with a memorial flag. The family needs to make funeral arrangements with a funeral firm and have them transport the remains to the cemetery.

Regardless of where an honorably discharged veteran is buried, allowances may be available for the plot, and the burial and grave marker expenses. The amount varies depending on factors such as whether the veteran died because of a service related injury. The VA will not reimburse any burial or funeral expense for the spouse of a veteran.

For information about reimbursement of funeral and burial expenses you can call the VA at (800) 827-1000.

The Department of Veteran's Affairs has a Web site with information on the following topics:

> National and Military Cemeteries
> Burial, Headstones and Markers
> State Cemetery Grants Program
> Obtaining Military Records
> Locating Veterans

 VA CEMETERY WEB SITE
http://www.cem.va.gov

BENEFITS FOR SPOUSE OF DECEDENT VETERAN

SPOUSE

The surviving spouse of an honorably discharged veteran should contact the Veteran's Administration to determine whether he/she is eligible for any benefits. For example, if the decedent had minor or disabled children, his spouse may also be eligible for a monthly benefit of Dependency and Indemnity Compensation ("DIC"). If the Veteran's surviving spouse receives nursing home care under Medicaid, then the spouse might be eligible for monthly payments from the VA.

Whether a surviving spouse is eligible for any of these benefits depends on many factors including whether the decedent was serving on active duty, whether his death was service related, and the surviving spouse's assets and income. DIC benefits are discontinued should the surviving spouse remarry; however, a recent change in the law permits payments to be resumed, if the subsequent marriage end because of death or divorce.

For information about whether the surviving spouse is eligible for any benefit related to the decedent's military service call the VA at (800) 827-1000. You can receive a printed statement of public policy: VA Pamphlet 051-000-00217-2 FEDERAL BENEFITS FOR VETERANS AND DEPENDENTS by sending a check in the amount of $5 to

THE SUPERINTENDENT OF DOCUMENTS
P.O. Box 371954
Pittsburgh, PA 15250-7954

Information is also available at the VA Web site:

VA WEB SITE
http://www.va.gov

 **LAWYER** ## THE WRONGFUL DEATH

The decedent's surviving spouse and next of kin have the right to be compensated for any economic loss, including lost financial support, they suffer because of a ***wrongful death*** (a death caused by a wrongful act). They cannot sue directly but must ask the District Court to appoint a Trustee to do so. The Trustee will proceed with the wrongful death action and seek compensation for any financial loss suffered by the next of kin. The Trustee can also seek punitive damages if he can prove that there was a deliberate disregard for the rights or safety of the decedent (MN 549.20, 573.02).

If the death was caused by the negligence of a doctor, dentist, hospital or nursing home then the law suit must be filed within two years from the date of death. A wrongful death caused by anyone else can be filed within 3 years from the date of death, provided that the injury that caused the death happened not more than 6 years prior to the date of filing. There is no time limit for filing a wrongful death action if the decedent was murdered.

If the Trustee is successful and monies are awarded, the District Court will determine how the funds are to be distributed. The Court will order the funds be used to pay for the decedent's funeral expenses and the remainder distributed to the spouse and next of kin. The Court will make the distribution in proportion to the loss they suffered.

The State of Minnesota reimburses crime victims and/or their families, for loses that are not covered by insurance or any other compensation. If the decedent died because of a criminal act, his family members (spouse, domestic partner, former spouse, child, parent, grandparent or sibling) may be eligible to be reimbursed for economic losses they have suffered. Funds can be awarded for funeral and burial expenses, medical bills, mental health counseling and loss of support for dependents. Total compensation to all family members cannot exceed $50,000 (MN 611A.52, 611A.53, 611A.54).

The Minnesota Crime Victims Reparation Board implements the program and has established a set of rules to administer the program (Administrative Rules Chapter 3050). To receive an award, all of the following must be true:

➢ The decedent was an innocent victim.

➢ There was full cooperation with law enforcement officers by the victim and/or his family.

➢ The crime was reported within 30 days of discovery and application for compensation was filed within 3 years from the crime.

You can get an application to file a claim by calling (888) 622-8799 or you can write to:

MINNESOTA CRIME VICTIMS REPARATION BOARD
245 E. 6th Street, #705
St. Paul, MN   55101

You can download an application from the Internet.

 DEPARTMENT OF PUBLIC SAFETY
http://www.dps.state.mn.us

THE UNCLAIMED BODY

Police make every effort to identify and locate the family of an unclaimed body. If the body cannot be identified, or if no one can be found who will take responsibility for the disposition of the body, the county Medical Examiner has authority to offer the body to a school for anatomical study and research.

The Medical Examiner also has authority to make an anatomical gift of the body for transplantation or therapy, if he receives a request for the donation from medical personnel or the Organ Procurement Organization. The Medical Examiner may not make the donation if he knows that the decedent objected to donating his body for transplantation, or if any of the decedent's next of kin object.

If the decedent was indigent and the body is not suitable for donation, the Medical Examiner will arrange for the cremation or burial of the body. Payment for the cost of the final disposition is made by the County Board in the county where the death occurred (MN 383B.225, 525.9213).

THE INDIGENT VETERAN
Honorably discharged veterans who are indigent, can be buried without charge. All the family need do is contact the VA as explained on page 17, or they can call the local County Veteran Service Officer for assistance. The name and address for County Veteran Service Officers appears on Minnesota Department of Veteran Affairs Web site:

 MINNESOTA DEPARTMENT OF VETERAN AFFAIRS
http://www.mdva.state.mn.us

THE PROBLEM
FUNERAL OR BURIAL

The funeral and burial industry is well regulated by both state and federal government. Under Minnesota law, the following acts are subject to disciplinary action:

⊠ Soliciting business from a relative of someone whose death is imminent;

⊠ Paying kick-backs to generate business;

⊠ Using false, misleading or deceptive advertising, such as advertising the founding date of an established business when it recently has changed ownership;

⊠ Using profane, indecent or obscene language within the hearing of the family of the decedent;

⊠ Failing to treat the body of the decedent with dignity and respect (MN 149A.70).

Funeral directors are licensed professionals so it is unusual to have a problem with the funeral or burial or cremation. If, however, you had a bad experience with any aspect of the funeral you can call the Minnesota licensing agency at (651) 282-3829 or write to: Mortuary Science Section
121 E 7th Place
P.O. Box 64975
St. Paul, MN 55164-0975

In addition to filing a complaint with the state licensing agency, you may wish to consult with an attorney who is experienced in litigation matters to learn of any other legal remedy that you may have.

 **LAWYER** THE MISSING PERSON

Few things are more difficult to deal with than a missing person. The emotional turmoil created by the "not knowing" is often more difficult than the finality of death. The legal problems created by the disappearance are also more difficult than if the person simply died. It may take a two-part legal process to settle the estate — first appointing someone, a *Receiver* to take possession of the missing person's property during his absence; and then a final Probate proceeding if it is determined that the Absentee is dead.

APPOINTING THE RECEIVER

If a person has been missing for at least 3 months, and there are matters that need attending (family to be maintained, bills to be paid, etc.), any interested party (family member, creditor, insurance company, etc.) can *petition* (ask) the Probate Court in the county of the absentee's residence, for the appointment of a Receiver. Once appointed, the Court will issue orders directing the care and custody of the property in the possession of the Receiver.

After 4 years from the disappearance any interested party can ask Court to conduct a hearing to establish that the Absentee is dead. If the Court determines that the Absentee cannot be found after diligent search, the Court will issue an order declaring the Absentee to be dead and directing the Receiver to distribute the decedent's property to the proper beneficiaries (MN 576.04, 576.011, 576.12, 576.141, 576.142).

THE DEATH CERTIFICATE

It is the job of the funeral director or cremation service director to provide information about the decedent to the local Registrar (MN 149A.90). The Registrar will prepare a death certificate based on that information. It is important that the information you give to the funeral or cremation director is correct. It is also important that you check the form completed by the funeral or cremation director to be sure names are correctly spelled and dates correctly written. Once the information becomes part of the state's Vital Statistics, it will be difficult and time consuming to make a correction.

Most establishments require an original certified copy and not a photocopy so you need to order sufficient certified copies. The following is a list of institutions that may want a certified copy:

* Each insurance company that insured the decedent or his property (health insurance, life insurance, etc.)
* Each financial institution in which the decedent had money invested (brokerage houses, banks)
* The decedent's pension fund
* Each credit card company used by the decedent
* The IRS and the Minnesota Department of Revenue
* The Social Security Administration
* The Driver and Vehicle Services Bureau
* If a Probate proceeding is necessary, then the Clerk of the Probate Court.

Some airlines and car rental companies offer a discount for short notice, emergency trips. If you have family flying in for the funeral, you may wish to order a few extra copies of the death certificate so that they can obtain an airline or car rental discount.

ORDERING COPIES OF THE DEATH CERTIFICATE

The funeral director can order as many certified copies of the death certificate as you request. If you need a certified copy of the death certificate at a later date you can have your attorney or the funeral director order additional copies. If you wish you can obtain a copy from your local Registrar; however Minnesota law restricts access to a certified copy of the death certificate unless you are:

- ❀ the decedent's spouse, child, parent or grandparent
- ❀ the Personal Representative of the Estate
- ❀ the Trustee of the decedent's Trust
- ❀ anyone who is legally entitled to inherit the decedent's Estate (MN 144.225).

If you are one of these persons, you can get a copy from the local Registrar in the county of the decedent's residence. If the decedent was not a resident of Minnesota, you can get the death certificate in the county where the person died. You will need to produce identification and complete an application verifying that you need the certificate to settle the decedent's Estate. You can get the application and the address and telephone number of the County Registrar from the Department of Health Web site:

 MINNESOTA DEPARTMENT OF HEALTH
http://www.health.state.mn.us

BY MAIL: You can get a death certificate by writing to:
Minnesota Department of Health
P.O. Box 64975; St. Paul, MN 55164-0975
It is a good idea to first call them at (651) 215-5800 and have them mail you an application.

If you need a certified copy of the death certificate in order to present a claim to the Veteran's Administration, the Registrar will provide you with a certified copy, free of charge (MN 197.63).

About Probate

Once a person dies, all of the property he owns as of the date of his death is referred to as the **decedent's Estate.** If the decedent owned property that was in his name only (not jointly or in trust for someone) then some sort of court procedure may be necessary to determine who is entitled to possession of the property. The name of the court procedure is **Probate**. In most counties the County Court contains a Probate division. In Hennepin and Ramsey counties, the District Court is also the Probate Court (MN 484.011, 487.01, 487.27). We will refer to the Court that conducts the Probate proceeding as the **Probate Court**.

The root of the word Probate is "to prove." It refers to the first job of the Probate Court, that is, to examine proof of whether the decedent left a valid Will. The second job of the Probate Court is to appoint someone, to be the decedent's **Personal Representative** who will wrap up the affairs of the decedent by paying any outstanding bill and then distributing what property is left to the proper beneficiary.

If the decedent left a valid Will naming someone as **Executor** of his Estate, then the Court will appoint that person for the job and issue **Letters Testamentary** giving him authority to administer the estate. If the decedent died without a Will, then the Probate Court will appoint someone to be the **Administrator** of the Estate and issue **Letters of Administration** (MN 524.1-201).

For simplicity, we will refer to the person appointed by the court to settle the decedent's Estate as the **Personal Representative**, and the document authorizing him to act, as **Letters**.

There are different ways to conduct a Probate proceeding depending on the value of the property that is being Probated, and whether the decedent owned real property at the time of his death. We will refer to the property that is distributed as part of a Probate proceeding as the decedent's **Probate Estate** and the method of conducting a Probate proceeding as the **Estate Administration**. Chapter 6 explains the different kinds of Estate Administration that are available in the state of Minnesota.

But we are getting ahead of ourselves. First we need to determine whether a Probate proceeding is necessary. To answer that question we need to know exactly what the decedent owned, so the next two chapters explain how to identify, and then locate, all of the decedent's assets.

Giving Notice Of The Death 2

Those closest to the decedent usually notify family members and close friends by telephone. The funeral director will arrange to have an obituary published in as many different newspapers as the family requests, but there is still the job of notifying the government and people who were doing business with the decedent. That job is the duty of whoever is appointed as Personal Representative of the decedent's Estate.

Minnesota law gives an order of priority for the appointment of Personal Representative. Whoever the decedent named as Personal Representative in his Will has top priority. If the decedent died *intestate* (without a Will), the decedent's spouse has priority to be appointed as Personal Representative, so it is the job of the surviving spouse to let every one know of the death (MN 524.3-203).

If there is no spouse, the job falls to his next of kin. By *next of kin,* we mean those people who inherit the decedent's property according to Minnesota's LAWS OF INTESTATE SUCCESSION. That law is explained in Chapter 5.

NOTIFYING SOCIAL SECURITY

Many funeral directors will, as part of their service package, notify the Social Security Administration of the death. You may wish to check to see that this has been done. You can do so by calling (800) 772-1213. If you are hearing impaired call (800) 325-0778 TTY. You will need to give the Social Security Administration the full legal name of the decedent as well as his social security number and date of birth.

 Special Situation

DECEDENT RECEIVING SOCIAL SECURITY CHECKS

If the decedent was receiving checks from Social Security, then you need to determine whether his last check needs to be returned to the Social Security Administration.

Each Social Security check is a payment for the prior month, provided that person lives for the entire prior month. If someone dies on the last day of the month, then you should not cash the check for that month. For example, if someone dies on July 31st, then you need to return the check that the agency mails out in August. If however, the decedent died on August 1st then the check sent in August need not be returned because that check is payment for the month of July.

If the Social Security check is electronically deposited into a bank account, then notify the bank that the account holder died and notify the Social Security Administration as well. If the check needs to be returned, then the Social Security Administration will withdraw it electronically from the bank account. You will need to keep the account open until the funds are withdrawn.

SPOUSE	SPOUSE/CHILD'S SOCIAL SECURITY BENEFITS

If the decedent had sufficient work credits, the Social Security Administration will give the decedent's widow(er) or if unmarried, then the decedent's minor children, a one-time death benefit of $255.

SURVIVORS BENEFITS:

The spouse (or ex-spouse) of the decedent may be eligible for Survivors Benefits. Benefits vary depending on the amount of work credits earned by the decedent; whether the decedent had minor or disabled children; the spouse's age; how long they were married; etc. The minor child of the decedent may be eligible for benefits regardless of whether the child's father (the decedent) ever married the child's mother. Paternity can be established by any one of several methods including the father acknowledging his child in writing or verbally to members of his family. For more information you can call the Social Security Administration at (800) 772-1213.

SOCIAL SECURITY BENEFITS

A spouse or ex-spouse can collect social security benefits based on the decedent's work record. This value may be greater than the spouse now receives. It is important to make an appointment with your local Social Security office and determine whether you as the spouse (or ex-spouse) or parent of decedent's minor child are eligible for any Social Security or Survivor benefit. The Social Security Administration has a Web site from which you can down load publications that explain survivors benefits:

SOCIAL SECURITY WEB SITE
http://www.ssa.gov

DECEDENT WITH GOVERNMENT PENSION

Any pension or annuity check received after the date of death of a federal retiree, or a survivor annuitant, needs to be returned to the U.S. Treasury. If the check is direct deposited to a bank account, then call the financial institution and ask them to return the check. If the check is sent by mail then you need to return it to:

Director, Regional Finance Center
U. S. Treasury Department
P.O. Box 7367
Chicago, IL 60680

Include a letter explaining the reason for the return of the check and stating the decedent's date of death.

$$$ APPLY FOR BENEFITS $$$

A survivor annuity may be available to a surviving spouse, and/or minor or disabled child. In some cases, a former spouse may be eligible for benefits. Even though you notify the government of the death, they will not automatically give you benefits to which you may be entitled. You need to apply for those benefits by notifying the Office of Personnel Management ("OPM") of the death and requesting that they send you an application for survivor benefits. You can call them at **(888) 767-6738** or you can write to:

THE OFFICE OF PERSONNEL MANAGEMENT
SERVICE AND RECORDS CENTER
BOYERS, PA 16017

You will find brochures and information about Survivor's Benefits at the OPM Web site:

 OFFICE OF PERSONNEL MANAGEMENT WEB SITE
http://www.opm.gov

DECEDENT WITH COMPANY PENSION OR ANNUITY

In most cases, pension and annuity checks are payment for the prior month. If the decedent received his pension or annuity check before his death, then no monies need be returned. Pension checks and/or annuity checks received after the date of death may need to be returned to the company. You need to notify the company of the death to determine the status of the last check sent to the decedent.

Before notifying the company, locate the policy or pension statement that is the basis of the income. That document should tell whether there is a beneficiary of the pension or annuity funds now that the pensioner or annuitant is dead. If you cannot locate the document, use the return address on the check envelope and ask the company to send you a copy of the plan. Also request that they forward to you any claim form that may be required in order for the survivor or beneficiary to receive benefits under that pension plan or policy.

If the pension/annuity check is direct deposited to the decedent's account, then ask the bank to assist you in locating the company and notifying the company of the death.

Anyone who is a beneficiary of an Individual Retirement Account ("IRA") or QRP needs to keep in mind that no income taxes have been paid on monies placed in an IRA or QRP account. Once monies are withdrawn, significant taxes may be due. You need to learn what options are available to you as a beneficiary of the plan and the tax consequences of each option. You will need to ask an accountant how much will be due in taxes for each option. Once you know all the facts, you will be able to make the best choice for your circumstance.

SPOUSE

If the spouse is the beneficiary of the decedent's IRA account, then there are special options available. The spouse has the right to withdraw the money from the account or roll it over into the spouse's own retirement account. Although the employer can explain options that are available, the spouse still needs to understand the tax consequence of choosing any given option. It is important to consult with an accountant, or a financial planner to determine the best way to go.

If the decedent had a QRP, the plan may permit the spouse to roll the balance of the account into a new IRA. The spouse needs to contact the decedent's employer for an explanation of the plan and all the options that are available at this time.

NOTIFYING IRS

THE FINAL INCOME TAX RETURN

The decedent's final income tax return (IRS form 1040) needs to be filed by April 15th of the year following the year in which he died. The state income tax is filed at the same time. If the decedent was married, the surviving spouse can file a final joint return. If a Probate proceeding is necessary, the Personal Representative can choose to file the return jointly with the spouse or individually on behalf of the decedent. If the return is filed jointly, the Personal Representative and the surviving spouse are equally responsible to pay the tax; however any refund will be sent to the surviving spouse. If there is no surviving spouse, then it is the Personal Representative's job to file the decedent's final income tax returns (MN 289A.18, 524.3-715).

If no Probate proceeding is necessary, and the value of the Probate Estate is less than $20,000, the decedent's child, grandchild, parent, brother or sister, niece or nephew may file the decedent's final return. You can get forms for filing by calling the Individual Income Tax Division at (800) 627-3529 or you can download forms and get information about filing from the Internet.

 MINNESOTA DEPARTMENT OF REVENUE
http:www.taxes.state.mn.us

If you have a joint account with the decedent, you may want to keep it open until you determine whether the decedent is entitled to an income tax refund. See Chapter 6 for an explanation of how to obtain a refund from the IRS.

THE GOOD NEWS

Monies inherited from the decedent are generally not counted as income to you, so you do not pay federal income tax on those monies. If the monies you inherit later earn interest or income for you, then of course you will report that income as you do any other type of income.

| SPOUSE | SELLING THE HOME

In the tough "ole days" the IRS used to allow a Capital Gains Tax exclusion (up to $125,000) on the sale of one's **homestead** (the principal residence). A person had to be 55 or older to take advantage of the exclusion, and it was a once-in-a-lifetime tax break. If a married couple sold their home and took the exclusion it was "used up" and no longer available to either partner.

In these, the good times, the IRS allows you to sell your home and up to $250,000 ($500,000 for a married couple) of the home-sale profit is tax free. There is no limit on the number of times you can use the Capital Gains Tax Exclusion, provided you own and live in the home at least two years prior to the sale (IRC Section 121 (b) 3).

If, under the old law, the decedent and his spouse used their "once in a lifetime" homestead tax exclusion, with this new law, the surviving spouse can sell the homestead and once again take advantage of a tax break.

BENEFICIARY OF A
MINNESOTA HOMESTEAD

A Minnesota resident who owns and occupies his home is entitled to a reduction in his real estate taxes. Once the county Assessor gives the property a Homestead Classification, the Minnesota resident is entitled to a significant tax break. The Assessor will reclassify the decedent's homestead when it is transferred to an new owner, unless the owner files a homestead application requesting a Homestead Classification (MN 273.13, 273.124, 273.135).

In addition to the Homestead Classification certain property tax refunds are allowed for those home owners whose total household income is not greater than \$77,519 per year. Subtractions from the household income are allowed for dependents, and for those over 65, or those who are blind or disabled. If you have inherited Minnesota property that you now occupy as your principal residence, and you believe you may be eligible for a refund, you need to apply for a refund on or before August 15th of the year in which the property taxes are due (MN 289A.18, 290A.04).

You get information about the Homestead Classification and how to file for a refund by calling the Minnesota Revenue Assistance line at (651) 296-3781 or (800) 654-9094. For the hearing impaired using a TTY machine, call (651) 297-2196. You can also get information and download forms from the Minnesota Revenue Web site:

MINNESOTA DEPARTMENT OF REVENUE
http:www.taxes.state.mn.us

AN ESTATE TAX FOR THE WEALTHY

Both the federal and state government have the right to impose an **Estate Tax** on property transferred to a beneficiary as a result of the death. All the property owned as of the date of death becomes the decedent's **Taxable Estate.** This includes real property (homestead, vacant lots, etc.) and personal property (cars, life insurance policies, business interests, securities, IRA accounts, etc.). It includes property held in the decedent's name alone, as well as property that he held jointly or in Trust. It also includes gifts given by the decedent during his lifetime that exceeded $10,000 per person, per year. That **Annual Gift Tax Exclusion** is now based on the cost of living index and for 2002 is increased to $11,000.

For most of us, this is not a concern because no federal Estate Tax need be paid unless the decedent's Taxable Estate exceeds the federal **Estate Tax Exclusion** amount. That value is currently one million dollars and is scheduled to go even higher:

YEAR	ESTATE TAX EXCLUSION AMOUNT
2002-2003	$1,000,000
2004-2005	$1,500,000
2006-2008	$2,000,000
2009	$3,500,000

In 2010 the federal Estate Tax is scheduled to be phased out altogether; however in 2011, the Estate Tax will be reinstated unless lawmakers change the tax law once again.

There is an unlimited marital tax deduction for property transferred to the surviving spouse; so in most cases, no Estate tax need be paid if the decedent was married. Regardless of whether taxes are due, federal and state Estate tax returns must be filed whenever the decedent's Estate exceeds the federal Estate Tax Exclusion Amount in effect as of his date of death.

THE UN-UNIFIED GIFT TAX

Up until the year 2002, if you gave someone more than $10,000 in any given year you had to report that gift to the IRS. The Annual Gift Tax Exclusion is now adjusted for the cost of living and is $11,000 for the year 2002. The IRS keeps a running count of amounts that you give over the Annual Gift Tax Exclusion. Although you are required to report the gift, no tax need be paid unless that running total is more than the federal Estate Tax Exclusion amount. If your running total does not exceed that amount during your lifetime, once you die, the cumulative value of gifts reported to the IRS will be added to your Taxable Estate.

Up until the change in the tax law in 2001, the Gift and Estate tax were unified. No Gift Tax needed to be paid unless the total value of the taxable gifts exceeded the federal Estate Tax Exclusion amount. That changes in 2004. In 2004, the Estate Tax Exclusion amount goes up to $1,500,000, but the amount for the Gift Tax Exclusion remains at $1,000,000, so they are no longer unified.

To summarize:
If you make a gift to anyone that is greater than the Annual Gift Tax Exclusion for that year, you must report the gift the IRS. The IRS will keep count of values that you gave in excess of the Annual Gift Tax Exclusion. In 2004, if that sum exceeds $1,000,000, you will pay a Gift Tax on any amount that you give that is over the Annual Gift Tax Exclusion.

The Estate Tax is scheduled to be repealed in 2010, but not the Gift Tax.

The current federal Estate tax is scheduled to be phased out in the year 2010, but a new Capital Gains Tax is scheduled for 2010 that may prove even more costly than the Estate Tax. The new Capital Gains tax is related to the way inherited property is evaluated by the federal government. Real and personal property is inherited at a "step up" in basis, meaning that if the decedent's property has increased in value from the time he acquired it, the beneficiary will inherit the property at its fair market value as of the decedent's date of death. For example, if the decedent bought stock for $20,000 and it is worth $50,000 as of his date of death, the beneficiary will take a step-up in basis of $30,000; i.e. the beneficiary inherits the stock at the current $50,000 value. If the beneficiary sells the stock for $50,000, he pays no Capital Gains tax. If the beneficiary holds onto the stock and later sells it for $60,000, the beneficiary will pay a Capital Gains tax only on the $10,000 increase in value since the decedent's death.

Up to 2009, there is no limit to the amount a beneficiary can take as a step-up in basis. But in 2010 caps are set in place. The decedent's Estate will be allowed a 1.3 million dollar step-up in basis, plus another 3 million for property passing to the surviving spouse. The new law could result in significant Capital Gains taxes that the beneficiary must pay. For example, suppose in 2010 you inherit a business from your father that he purchased for $100,000 and it is now worth 2 million dollars. There is a capital gain of 1.9 million dollars, but you are allowed a step-up in basis of only 1.3 million. If you sell it for 2 million dollars $600,000 of your inheritance will be subject to a Capital Gains tax.

DECEDENT WITH A TRUST

If the decedent was the Grantor (or Settlor) of a Trust, then he was probably managing the Trust as Trustee during his lifetime. The Trust document should name a **Successor Trustee** to manage the Trust now that the Grantor is deceased. The Trust document may instruct the Successor Trustee to make certain gifts once the Grantor dies or the Trust document may direct the Successor Trustee to hold money in Trust for a beneficiary of the Trust.

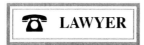

IF YOU ARE SUCCESSOR TRUSTEE

If you are the Successor Trustee then in addition to following the terms of the Trust, you are required to obey all of the laws of the state of Minnesota relating to the administration of the Trust. You should consult with an attorney experienced in Estate Planning to help you administer the Trust according to the law and without any liability to yourself.

IF YOU ARE A BENEFICIARY

If you are a beneficiary of the Trust, then you need to obtain a copy of the Trust provisions that apply to you and learn how the Trust will be administered now that the Grantor or Settlor is deceased. Most Trust documents are written in "legalese," so you may want to employ your own attorney to review the Trust, and explain your rights under that Trust.

NOTIFYING THE BUSINESS COMMUNITY

People and companies who were doing business with the decedent need to be notified of his death. This includes utility companies, banks, brokerage firms and any company that insured the decedent.

NOTIFY INSURANCE COMPANIES

Examine the decedent's financial records to determine the name and telephone number of all of the companies that insured the decedent or his property. This includes real property insurance, motor vehicle insurance, health insurance and life insurance.

MOTOR VEHICLE INSURANCE

Locate the insurance policy for all motor vehicles owed by the decedent (car, truck, boat, airplane; and notify the insurance company of the death. Determine how long insurance coverage continues after the death. Ask the insurance agent to explain what things are covered under the policy. Is the motor vehicle covered for all types of casualty (theft, accident, vandalism, etc.) or is coverage limited in some way?

If you can continue coverage, then determine when the next insurance payment is due. Hopefully, the car will be sold or transferred to a beneficiary before that date, but if not, you need to arrange for sufficient insurance coverage during the Probate proceeding.

LIFE INSURANCE COMPANIES

If the decedent had life insurance, you need to locate the policy and notify the company of his death. Call each life insurance company and ask what they require in order to forward the insurance proceeds to the beneficiary. Most companies will ask you to send them the original policy and a certified copy of the death certificate. Send the original policy by certified mail or any of the overnight services that require a signed receipt for the package. Make a copy of the original policy for your records before mailing the original policy to the company.

BANK ACCOUNT LIFE INSURANCE

Many banks, credit unions, savings and loan associations provide life insurance at no cost to the primary owner of the account. Such insurance is often overlooked when settling the decedent's affairs. Even though the amounts are generally small ($1,000 to $5,000), they can add up if the decedent had several accounts in different places. Contact each financial institution to determine whether such insurance is provided by the company.

IF YOU CANNOT LOCATE THE POLICY

If you know that the decedent was insured, but you cannot locate the insurance policy, you can contact the company and request a copy of the policy. A tougher question is how to locate the policy if you can't find the policy and do not know the name of the insurance company. The American Council of Life Insurers offers suggestions that you may find helpful at the Missing Policy Inquiry page of their Web site:

 AMERICAN COUNCIL OF LIFE INSURERS WEB SITE
http://www.acli.com

IF YOU CANNOT LOCATE THE COMPANY

If you cannot locate the insurance company it may be doing business under another name or it may no longer be doing business in the state of Minnesota. Each state has a branch of government that regulates insurance companies doing business in that state. If you are having difficulty locating the insurance company call the Department of Insurance in the state where the policy was purchased and ask for assistance in locating the company. In Minnesota, you can call the Office of the Insurance Commissioner at (651) 296-2488.

EAGLE PUBLISHING COMPANY OF BOCA has the telephone number for the Department of Insurance for each state at their Web site:

EAGLE PUBLISHING COMPANY OF BOCA WEB SITE
http://www.eaglepublishing.com

 *Special Situation*   ACCIDENTAL DEATH

If the decedent died as a result of an accident, then check for all possible sources of accident insurance coverage including his homeowner's policy. Some credit card companies provide accident insurance as part of their contract with their card holders.

If the decedent died in an automobile accident, check to see whether he was covered by any type of travel insurance, such as rental car insurance. If he belonged to an automobile club, such as AAA, then check whether he had accident insurance as part of his club membership.

HOMEOWNER'S INSURANCE

If the decedent owned his own home, then check whether there is sufficient insurance coverage on the property. The decedent may have neglected to increase his insurance as the property appreciated in value. If you think the property may be vacant for some period of time, then it is important to have vandalism coverage included in the policy. Once the property is sold, or transferred to the proper beneficiary, you can have the policy discontinued or transferred to the new owner. The decedent's Estate should receive a refund for the unused portion of the premium.

MORTGAGE INSURANCE

If the decedent had a mortgage on any parcel of real estate that he owned, he might have arranged with his lender for an insurance policy that pays off the mortgage balance in the event of his death. Look at the closing statement to see if there was a charge for mortgage insurance. Also check with the lender to determine if such a policy was purchased.

If the decedent was the sole owner of the property, then the beneficiary of that property needs to make arrangements to continue payment of the mortgage until title to the property is transferred to that beneficiary.

NOTIFY THE HOMEOWNER'S ASSOCIATION

If the decedent owned a condominium or a residence regulated by a homeowner's association, then the association will need to be notified of the death. Once the property is transferred to the proper beneficiary, he/she will need to contact the association to learn the rules and regulations regarding ownership and to arrange to have notices of dues and assessments forwarded to the new owner.

WORK RELATED INSURANCE

If the decedent was employed, then check his records for information about work related benefits. He may have survivor benefits from a company or group life insurance plan and/or a retirement plan. Also check with the employer about company benefits. If the decedent belonged to a union, then contact them to determine whether there are any union benefits.

The decedent may have belonged to a professional, fraternal or social organization such as the local Chamber of Commerce, a Veteran's organization, the Kiwanis, AARP, the Rotary Club, etc. If he belonged to any such organization check to see whether the organization provided any type of insurance coverage.

Special Situation > **BUSINESS OWNED BY DECEDENT**

If the decedent owned his own company or was a partner in a company he may have been covered by "key man" insurance. Key man insurance is a policy designed to protect the company should a valuable employee become disabled or die. Benefits are paid to the company to compensate the company for the loss of someone who is essential to the continuation of the business. Ultimately the policy benefits those who inherit the business.

If the decedent had an ownership interest in an ongoing business (sole proprietor, shareholder or partner) there may be a shareholder's or partnership agreement requiring the company to purchase the decedent's share of the business. The Personal Representative or his attorney needs to investigate to see if there was a key man insurance policy and/or such purchase agreement.

Special Situation

CORPORATE OWNER OR REGISTERED AGENT

If the decedent was the sole owner of a corporation and the company stock was in his name only, then there may need to be a Probate proceeding in order to transfer the company to the new owner.

Minnesota law requires each corporation authorized to do business in the state to continuously maintain a Registered Office in this state. If the decedent was the sole officer or Registered Agent of the company, then the Minnesota Secretary of State needs to be notified of the new Registered Office or Registered Agent as soon as is practicable (MN 317A.121, 317A.123).

Forms to provide notice of the change of officers, directors and Registered Agent can be obtained by calling (877) 551-6767 or by writing to:

Minnesota Secretary of State
180 State Office Building, 100 Constitution Avenue
St. Paul, MN   55155

If you were not actively involved in running the business, then you might request a status report of the company. The report will show whether filing fees are current and will identify the officers and directors of the company.

You can get information about the corporation and download forms to change the Registered Office from the Secretary of State Web site.

 MINNESOTA SECRETARY OF STATE
http://www.sos.state.mn.us/

NOTIFY ADVERTISERS

Probably the last in the world to learn of the decedent's death is the direct mail advertiser. Advertisers are nothing if not tenacious. It is not uncommon for advertisements to be mailed to the decedent for more than ten years after the death. It is not because the advertiser is trying to sell something to the decedent, but rather the people who prepare (and sell) mailing lists do not know that the person is dead.

Those who sell mailing lists may not be motivated to update the list because of the cost of doing the necessary research; and maybe even because the price of the mailing list is often based on the number of people on the list. Even those who compose their own list may decide it is less costly to mail to everyone, than take the time (and money) to update the list.

If it gives you pleasure to think of advertisers spending substantial sums for nothing, then that is what you should do (nothing). But for those of you who wince each time you see another piece of mail addressed to the decedent, you can write to the Direct Marketing Association and ask that the name be deleted from all mailing lists:

> Mail Preference Service
> Direct Marketing Association
> P.O. Box 9008
> Farmingdale, NY 11735

You will need to give them the decedent's complete address, including zip code and every name variation that the decedent may have used; for example:

> Mr. Theodore James Jones
> Ted Jones   Ted J. Jones
> T. J. Jones   T. James Jones, etc.

HEALTH INSURANCE

The Health Insurance carrier probably knows of the death, but it is a good idea to contact them to determine what coverage the decedent had under that insurance plan. If you cannot find the original policy, have the insurance company send you a copy of the policy so that you can determine whether medical treatment given to the decedent before his death was covered by that policy.

 *Special Situation* **DECEDENT ON MEDICARE**

If the decedent was covered by Medicare, you do not need to notify anyone, but you do need to know what things were covered by Medicare so that you can determine what medical bills are (or are not) covered by Medicare.

The government publication **MEDICARE AND YOU** (Publication No. CMS-11007) explains what things are covered under Medicare. You can get the publication by writing to:

U.S. Dept. of Health and Human Services
Centers for Medicare and Medicaid Services
7500 Security Boulevard
Baltimore, MD 21244-1850

You can also find the publication on the Internet:

 MEDICARE WEB SITE
http:/www.medicare.gov

THE SPOUSE'S
| SPOUSE | HEALTH INSURANCE

If the spouse of the decedent is insured under Medicare, then the death does not affect the surviving spouse's coverage. If spouse was not covered by Medicare but has her own health insurance that also covered the decedent, then the spouse needs to notify the employer of the death because this may affect the cost of the plan to the employer and/or the spouse.

If the spouse was covered under the decedent's policy then he/she needs to arrange for new coverage. There are state and federal laws that ensure continued coverage under the decedent's policy for a period of time depending on whether the decedent's employer falls under federal or state regulation.

If the decedent was employed by a federally regulated company (usually a company with at least twenty employees) then under the Consolidated Omnibus Budget Reconciliation Act ("COBRA") the employer must make the company health plan available to the surviving spouse and any dependent child of the decedent for at least 36 months. The employer is required to give notice to the surviving spouse that the spouse and/or dependent child have the right to continue coverage under the decedent's health plan.

The spouse and/or child have 60 days from the date of death or 60 days after the employer sends notice (whichever is later) to tell the employer whether the surviving spouse and child wish to continue with the health insurance plan (29 USC 18 Sec. 1162, 1163).

SPOUSE'S HEALTH INSURANCE (continued)

The only problem with continued coverage may be the cost. Before the death, the employer may have been paying some percentage of the premium. The employer has no such duty after the death unless there was some employment agreement stating otherwise. Under COBRA, the employer may charge the spouse for the full cost of the plan plus a 2% administrative fee.

If you have a question about your coverage under COBRA, you can call the U.S. Department of Labor ("DOL") at (800) 998-7542 and ask for the number of your local DOL office. You can also ask that they send you their publication HEALTH BENEFITS UNDER COBRA; or you can visit their Web site for more information:

 DEPARTMENT OF LABOR WEB SITE
http://www.dol.gov/dol/pwba

CONTINUED COVERAGE UNDER STATE LAW
Minnesota law regulates plans offered by health insurance carriers to small employers. Under Minnesota law, small employer plans must include the same continued coverage provisions as required by COBRA (MN 62L.05).

CHANGE BENEFICIARIES

If the decedent was someone you named as beneficiary of your insurance policy, Will or Trust, brokerage account or pension plan, then you may need to name another beneficiary in his place:

INSURANCE POLICY

If you named the decedent as the primary beneficiary of your life insurance policy, then check to see whether you named a ***contingent*** (alternate) beneficiary in the event that the decedent did not survive you. If not, then you need to contact the insurance company and name a new beneficiary. If you did name a contingent beneficiary, then that person is now your primary beneficiary and you need to consider whether you wish to name a new contingent beneficiary at this time.

HEALTH INSURANCE POLICY

If the decedent was covered under your health insurance policy, then your employer and the health insurer need to be notified of the death because this may affect the cost of the plan to you and/or your employer.

WILL OR TRUST

Most Wills provide for a contingent beneficiary in the event that the person named as beneficiary dies first. If you named the decedent as your beneficiary, then check to see whether you named an alternate (or contingent) beneficiary. If not, you need to have your attorney revise your Will and name a new beneficiary.

Similarly, if you are the Grantor or Settlor of a Trust and the decedent was one of the beneficiaries of your Trust, then check the Trust document to see if you named an alternate beneficiary. If not, contact your attorney to prepare an amendment to the Trust, naming a new beneficiary.

BANK AND SECURITIES ACCOUNTS ✍

If the decedent was a beneficiary of your bank or securities account, or if the decedent was a joint owner of your bank account or securities account, then it is important to contact the financial institution and tell them about the death. You may wish to arrange for a new beneficiary or joint owner at this time.

PENSION PLANS ✍

If the decedent was a beneficiary under your pension plan, then you need to notify them of his death and name a new beneficiary. Many pension plans require that you notify them within a set period of time (usually 30 days) so it is important to notify them as soon as you are able. If the decedent was a beneficiary of your Individual Retirement Account ("IRA") or of your Qualified Retirement Plan ("QRP") and you did not provide for an alternate beneficiary, then you need to name someone at this time.

Before you choose an alternate beneficiary, it is important that you understand all of the options available to you. Not an easy task. There are many complex government regulations relating to IRA and QRP accounts. And even if you believe you understood your options when you set up your account, they are scheduled to be changed beginning in 2002. You can read about the proposed regulations under 42 U.S.C 401(a)(9) in the *Federal Register* that was published on January 17, 2001, but unless you have an extensive tax background, it is just so much "legalese," i.e., incomprehensible without a professional to translate it into plain English.

Your choice of beneficiary can impact the amount of money you can withdraw each month, so it is important to consult with your accountant or tax attorney or financial planner, before you make your election.

NOTIFY CREDIT CARD COMPANIES

You need to notify the decedent's credit card companies of the death. If you can find the contract with the credit card company check to see whether the decedent had credit card insurance. If the decedent had credit card insurance, then the balance of the account is now paid in full. If you cannot find the contract contact the company and get a copy of the contract along with a statement of the balance due as of the date of death.

DESTROY DECEDENT'S CREDIT CARDS

You need to destroy all of the decedent's credit cards. If you hold a credit card jointly with the decedent, then it is important to waste no time in closing that account and opening another in your name only.

That's something Barbara knows from hard experience. She and Hank never married but they did live together for several years before he died from liver disease. Hank came from a well to do family so he had enough money to support himself and Barbara during his long illness. Hank put Barbara on all of his credit card accounts so that she could purchase things when he became too ill to go shopping with her. After the funeral, Barbara had a gathering of friends and family at their apartment. Barbara was so preoccupied with her loss that she never noticed that Hank's credit cards were missing until the bills started coming in.

Barbara did not know who ran up the bills on Hank's credit cards during the month following his death. It was obvious that Hank's signature had been forged — but who forged it? One credit card company suspected that it might have been Barbara herself to get out of paying the bill by saying that the card had been stolen.

Because the cards were held jointly, Barbara became liable to either pay the charges to the credit card or to prove that she did not make the purchases. She was able to clear her credit record but it took several months and she had to employ an attorney to do so.

NOTIFYING OTHER CREDITORS

If a Probate proceeding is necessary and the decedent owed money, then it is the job of the person appointed as Personal Representative to notify the decedent's creditors of the death. The attorney who handles the Probate will explain to the Personal Representative how notice is to be given.

If no Probate proceeding is necessary, then the next of kin can notify the creditors of the death, but before doing so, read Chapter 4: WHAT BILLS NEED TO BE PAID? That chapter explains what bills need to be paid and who is responsible to pay them.

Before any bill can be paid you need to know whether the decedent left any assets that could be used to pay those debts. The next chapter explains how to identify, and then locate all of the property owned by the decedent.

Locating the Assets 3

It is important to locate the financial records of the decedent and then carefully examine those records. Even the partner of a long-term marriage should conduct a thorough search because the surviving spouse may be unaware of all that was owned (or owed) by the decedent.

It is not unusual for a surviving spouse to be surprised when learning of the decedent's business transactions, especially in those cases where the decedent had control of family finances. One such example is that of Sam and Henrietta. They married just as soon as Sam was discharged from the army after World War II. During their marriage, Sam handled all of the finances giving Henrietta just enough money to run the household.

Every now and again Henrietta would think of getting a job. She longed to have her own source of income and some economic independence. Each time she brought up the subject Sam would loudly object. He had no patience for this new "woman's lib" thing. Sam said he got married to have a real wife — one who would cook his meals and keep house for him.

Henrietta was not the arguing type. She rationalized, saying that Sam had a delicate stomach and dust allergies. He needed her to prepare his special meals and keep an immaculate house for him. Besides, Sam had a good job with a major cruise line and he needed her to accompany him on his frequent business trips.

Once Sam retired, he was even more cautious in his spending habits. Henrietta seldom complained. She assumed the reason for his "thrift" was that they had little money and had to live on his pension.

They were married 52 years when Sam died at the age of 83. Henrietta was 81 at the time of his death. She was one very happy, very angry and very aged widow when she discovered that Sam left her with assets worth well over a million dollars!

LOCATING RECORDS

As you go through the papers of the decedent you may come across documents that indicate property ownership, such as bank account statements, stock or bond certificates, insurance policies, brokerage account statements, etc. Place all evidence of ownership in a single place. You will need to contact the different companies in order to transfer title to the proper beneficiary. Chapter 5 explains how to identify the proper beneficiary of the decedent's property. Chapter 6 explains how to transfer the property to that beneficiary.

You may also need to produce evidence of the decedent's personal relationships, such as a marriage certificate, birth certificate, or naturalization papers, a Final Judgement of Divorce, military personnel records, etc. If you cannot locate his marriage certificate or birth certificate, you can get a certified copy of those records from the County Registrar's office in the county where the event took place. See page 25 for the Web site of the Department of Health. That site gives the location of the Registrar's office for each county in Minnesota. You can use your Internet search engine to locate the Vital Statistics or Vital Records offices of other states.

For deceased veterans, you can obtain a copy of his military record by writing to:

The National Personnel Records Center
Military Personnel Records
9700 Page Avenue
St. Louis, MO   63132-5100

They will send you form SF 180 to complete. You can get the form from the Internet at http://www.cem.va.gov or from the National Archives and Records Administration Fax-On-Demand system. Dial (301) 713-6905 and request document number 2255.

COLLECT AND IDENTIFY KEYS

The decedent may have kept his records in a safe deposit box, so you may find that your first job is to locate the keys to the box. As you go through the personal effects of the decedent, collect and identify all the keys that you find. If you come across an unidentified key, it could be a key to a post office box (private or federal) or a safe deposit box located in a bank or in a private vault company. You will need to determine whether that key opens a box that contains property belonging to the decedent or whether the key is to a box no longer in use. Some ways to investigate are as follows:

☑ **CHECK BUSINESS RECORDS**

If the decedent kept receipts, look through those items to see if he paid for the rental of a post office or safe deposit box. Also, look at his check register to see if he wrote a check to the Postmaster or to any safe deposit or vault company. Look at his bank statements to see if there is any bank charge for a safe deposit box. Some banks bill separately for safe deposit boxes so check with all of the banks in which the decedent had an account to determine whether he had a safe deposit box with that bank.

☑ **CHECK THE KEY TYPE**

If you cannot identify the key take the key to all of the local locksmiths and ask whether anyone can identify the type of facility that uses such keys. If that doesn't work, then go to each bank, post office and private safe deposit box company where the decedent shopped, worked or frequented and ask whether they use the type of key that you found.

☑ **CHECK THE MAIL**

Check the mail over the next several months to see if the decedent receives a statement requesting payment for the next year's rental of a post office or safe deposit box.

You may find evidence of a brokerage account, bank account, or safe deposit box by examining correspondence addressed to the decedent. If the decedent was living alone, then have the mail forwarded to the person he named as Personal Representative of his Will. If the decedent did not leave a Will, and no Personal Representative has been appointed, then have the mail forwarded to his next of kin. Call the Postmaster and ask him/her to send you the necessary forms to make the change. Request that the mail be forwarded for the longest period allowed by law (currently one year).

The decedent may have been renting a post office box at his local post office branch or perhaps at the branch closest to where he did his banking. Ask the Postmaster to help you determine whether the decedent was renting a post office box. If so, then you need to locate the key to the box so that you can collect the decedent's mail.

 LOST POST OFFICE BOX KEY

If the decedent had a post office box and you cannot locate the key, then contact the local postmaster and ask him/her what documentation is needed for you to gain possession of the mail in that box. As before, you will ask the Postmaster to have all future mail addressed to that box, forwarded to the Personal Representative, or if no Probate proceeding has been started, then to the decedent's next of kin.

WHAT TO DO WITH CHECKS

You may receive checks in the mail made out to the decedent. Social security checks, pension checks and annuity checks issued after the date of death need to be returned to the sender. (See pages 28 and 30 of this book.) Other checks need to be deposited. If a Probate proceeding is necessary, then the Personal Representative will open a Probate Estate account and the checks should be deposited to that account.

If no Probate proceeding is necessary, then the checks can be deposited to any account held in the name of the decedent. The decedent is not here to endorse the check, but you can deposit it to his account by writing his bank account number on the back of the check and printing beneath it "**FOR DEPOSIT ONLY.**"

The bank will accept such an endorsement and deposit the check into the decedent's account. If the check is significant in value and/or the decedent had different accounts that are accessible to different people, then there needs to be cooperation and a sense of fair play. If not, the dollar gain may not nearly offset the emotional turmoil. Such was the case with Gail. Her father made her a joint owner of his checking account to assist in paying his bills. He had macular degeneration and it was increasingly difficult for him to see. The father also had a savings account that was in his name alone.

Gail's brother, Ken, had a good paying job in California. Even though he lived at a distance, Ken, his wife and two children always spent the spring break with his father. Gail's good cooking added to the festivities. Each winter their father enjoyed leaving the cold behind him to spend a few weeks in the warmth of his family and the California sun.

One year, the father treated himself to a first class ticket to California. It cost several hundred dollars. Just before the departure date, the father had a heart attack and died. Gail called the airline to cancel the ticket. They refunded the money in a check made out to her father. She deposited the check to the joint account.

As part of the Probate proceeding, the money in the father's savings account was divided equally between Ken and his sister. Ken wondered what happened to the money from the airline tickets.

Gail explained "He paid for the tickets from the joint account, so I deposited the money back to that account. "

"Aren't you going to give me half?"

"Dad meant for me to have whatever was in that joint account. If he wanted you to have half of the money, he would have made you joint owner as well."

Ken didn't see it that way "That refund was part of Dad's Probate Estate. It should have been deposited to his savings account to be divided equally between us. Are you going force me to argue this in court?"

Gail finally agreed to split the money with Ken, but the damage was done.

Gail complains that the holidays are lonely since her father died.

LOCATING FINANCIAL RECORDS

To locate the decedent's assets you need to find evidence of what he owned and where those assets are located. His financial records should lead you to the location of all of his assets so your first job is to locate those records. The best place to start the search is in the decedent's home. Many people keep their financial records in a single place but it is important to check the entire house to be sure you did not miss something.

CHECK THE COMPUTER

Don't overlook that computer sitting silently in the corner. It may hold the decedent's check register and all of the decedent's financial records. The computer may be programmed to protect information. If you cannot access the decedent's records, you may need to employ a computer technician or computer consultant who will be able to print out all of the information on the hard drive of the computer. You can find such a technician or consultant by looking in the telephone book under
COMPUTER SUPPORT SERVICES   or
COMPUTER SYSTEM DESIGNS & CONSULTANTS.

LOCATE TITLE TO WATERCRAFT

In Minnesota, all watercraft must be titled. If the decedent owned a watercraft, you need to locate his Certificate of Title. The Commissioner of Natural Resources will not issue a license to a new owner to operate the watercraft until title to the watercraft has been transferred. If you cannot locate the title to the decedent's watercraft, the Personal Representative can request a duplicate title from the Commissioner by calling (888-646-6367). In many counties the Deputy Registrar of Motor Vehicles can help you obtain a duplicate title and transfer it to the proper beneficiary (MN 86B:825, 86B:850).

LOCATE TITLE TO MOTOR VEHICLE

In Minnesota, if monies are owed on a motor vehicle (car or mobile home), the lender takes possession of the original certificate of title until the loan is paid; the borrower receives a duplicate title. If you cannot find the original certificate of title, then it is either lost or monies are owed on the car and the lienholder has the original title. In Minnesota, the Commissioner of Public Safety is the Registrar of Motor Vehicles. He has appointed Deputy Registrars in each county. If you determine that the title is lost, you can go to the Deputy Registrar's Office in the county of the decedent's residence and obtain a duplicate certificate of title. Upon proof of death, they will give a duplicate title to the surviving spouse, or the Personal Representative, or to the beneficiary of the car. You can obtain a duplicate title and transfer the car to the proper beneficiary all at the same time, so you may want to postpone the trip until you are ready to transfer title. See Chapter 6 for information about how to transfer title to the car.

THE LEASED CAR

When you contact the Registrar, you may find that the car is leased and not owned by the decedent. In such case, you need to contact the lessor and get a copy of the lease agreement. Once you have the lease agreement, check to see whether the decedent had life insurance as part of the agreement. If he did, then the lease may now be paid in full. The Personal Representative (or next of kin, if no Probate is necessary) can send the death certificate to the leasing company with a copy of the contract and a letter requesting that the paid contract be transferred to the decedent's beneficiary. If the lease is not paid in full upon the decedent's death, arrangements will need to be made to satisfy the terms of the lease agreement. See Chapter 6 for information about transferring a leased car.

LOCATE CONTRACTS

If the decedent belonged to a health club or gym, he may have prepaid for the year. Look for the club contract. It will give the terms of the agreement. If you cannot locate the contract then contact the company for a copy of the agreement. If the contract was prepaid, then determine whether the agreement provides for a refund for the unused portion.

SERVICE CONTRACT

Many people purchase appliance service contracts to have their appliances serviced in the event that an appliance should need repair. If the decedent had a security system then he may have had a service contract with a company to monitor the system and contact the police in the event of a break-in.

If the decedent had a service contract, then you need to locate it and determine whether it can be assigned to the new owner of the property. If the contract is assignable, the new owner can reimburse the decedent's Estate for the unused portion. If the contract cannot be assigned, then once the property is transferred, try to obtain a refund for the unused portion of the contract.

Special Situation

DECEDENT'S RESIDENTIAL LEASE

If the decedent was renting his residence, then he may have a written lease agreement. It is important to locate the lease because the decedent's Estate may be responsible for payments under the lease. If you cannot locate the lease, then ask the landlord for a copy. If the landlord reports that there was no written lease, then verify that the decedent was on a month-to-month basis and work out a mutually agreeable time in which to vacate the premises.

If a written lease is in effect, then determine the end of the lease period, and whether there was a security deposit. Ask whether the landlord will agree to cancel the lease on the condition that the property is left in good condition. If the landlord says that the Estate is responsible to pay the balance of the lease, then it is prudent to have an attorney review the lease to determine what rights and responsibilities remain now that the tenant is deceased.

☎ LAWYER

DECEDENT'S ONGOING BUSINESS

If the decedent was the sole owner of a business, or if he owned a partnership interest in a business, the Personal Representative needs to contact the company accountant to obtain the company's business records. If there is a company attorney, then the attorney may be able to assist in obtaining the records. If you are a beneficiary of the Estate, consider consulting with your own attorney to determine what rights and responsibilities you may have in the business.

COLLECT TAX RECORDS

You will need to file the decedent's final state and federal income tax returns so you need to collect all of his tax records for the past 3 years. If you cannot locate his prior tax records, then check his personal telephone book and/or his personal bank register to see if he employed someone to prepare his taxes. If you can locate his tax preparer, then he/she should have a copy of those records.

If you are unable to locate the decedent's federal tax returns then they can be obtained from the IRS. The IRS will send copies of the decedent's tax filings to anyone who has a *fiduciary relationship* with the decedent. The IRS considers the following people to be a fiduciary:

➢ the person appointed as the Personal Representative of the decedent's Estate

➢ the successor trustee of the decedent's trust

➢ if the person died without a Will, whoever is legally entitled to possession of the decedent's property (see page 115 for Minnesota's Laws of Intestate Succession).

The fiduciary can receive copies of the decedent's tax filings by notifying IRS that he/she is acting in a fiduciary capacity, and then requesting the copies.

To notify the IRS of the fiduciary capacity file Form 56:
NOTICE CONCERNING FIDUCIARY RELATIONSHIP

To request the copies, file IRS Form 4506:
REQUEST FOR COPY OR TRANSCRIPT OF TAX FORM
Your accountant can file these forms for you or you can obtain the forms from the IRS by calling (800) 829-3676 or you can download them from the Internet:

IRS FORMS WEB SITE
http://www.irs.gov/forms_pubs/forms.html

LOCATE STATE INCOME TAX RETURN

If you cannot locate the decedent's state income tax return you can get a copy from the Minnesota Department of Revenue. If a Probate proceeding is necessary, then the Personal Representative can get the copy. If no Probate is necessary, and you are next of kin, then you can request a copy by calling (800) 652-9094 or you can write to:

Minnesota Department of Revenue
Mail Station 4400
St. Paul, MN 55146-440

You will need to complete Form **M-100 REQUEST FOR COPY OF TAX RETURN** in order to obtain a copy of the tax return. You can download the form from the Department of Revenue Web site:

 MINNESOTA DEPARTMENT OF REVENUE
http://www.taxes.state.mn.us

LOCATE OUT OF STATE ACCOUNTS

If the decedent had out of state bank or brokerage accounts, then you might be able to locate them if they mail out monthly or quarterly statements. Not all financial institutions do so, but all institutions are required to send out an IRS tax form 1099 each year giving the amount of interest earned on that account. Once the forms come in, you will learn the location of all of the decedent's active accounts.

FINDING LOST/ ABANDONED PROPERTY

If the decedent was forgetful, he may have money in a lost bank account or abandoned safe deposit box. Property that is unclaimed is turned over the to Minnesota's Commissioner of Commerce after a period of time as set by Minnesota law. For most items it is five years, but that time period could vary depending on the item. For example:

- 1 year for unclaimed wages;
- 1 year after a utility deposit or refund is payable;
- 3 years from last activity on a bank account;
- 5 years from date that the lease period expired on a safe deposit box rental;
- 15 years from the issuing date of a travelers check.

(MN 345.32, 345.34, 345.39)

Within one year of receipt of any abandoned item, the Commission will try to contact the owner by mail and will also publish notice in a newspaper in the county of the owner's last known address. After 3 years of receiving a security or a tangible item, the Commissioner will convert the item to cash; i.e., he will sell a security. If the abandoned item is tangible such as jewelry he will sell that item at auction. If the item is later claimed, the Commissioner will give the proceeds of the sale to the owner (or his heir) (MN 345.42, 345.47, 345.49).

You can determine whether there is a record identifying the decedent as the owner of abandoned property by calling (615) 296-2568; in state (800) 925-5668 or by writing to: Minnesota Department of Commerce
Unclaimed Property Division
85   7th Place East, Suite 600
St. Paul, MN   55101-3165

or by visiting their Web site:

 MINNESOTA UNCLAIMED PROPERTY DIVISION
http://www.commerce.state.mn.us

CLAIMS IN OTHER STATES

Each state has an agency or department that is responsible for handling lost, abandoned or unclaimed property located within that state. If the decedent had residences in other states, then call the **UNCLAIMED or ABANDONED PROPERTY** department of the state Treasury to see if the decedent has unclaimed property in that state. Eagle Publishing Company has all of these telephone numbers at their Web site (www.eaglepublishing.com). Many states have information about unclaimed property for that state on the Internet at the state Web site or at:

 UNCLAIMED PROPERTY WEB SITE
http://www.missingmoney.com

CLAIMS FOR DECEDENT VICTIMS OF HOLOCAUST

The New York State Banking Department has a special Claims Processing Office for Holocaust survivors or their heirs. The office processes claims for Swiss bank accounts that were dormant since the end of World War II. If the decedent was a victim of the Holocaust, you can get information about money that may be due to the decedent's Estate by calling (800) 695-3318.

CLAIMS FOR IRS TAX REFUNDS

The IRS reports that some 90,000 tax refund checks representing 67.4 million dollars were returned to them as being not deliverable. They keep the information on file and will forward the full amount once they locate the taxpayer. You can determine whether they are holding a check for the decedent by calling the IRS at (800) 829-1040.

COLLECT DEEDS

Collect deeds to all of the property owned by the decedent. In addition to the deed, look for other documents associated with to the title to the land such as an *Abstract of Title*. An Abstract of Title is a summary of the documents or facts appearing on the public record which affect title to the property. The Abstract will need to be updated once the property is transferred. We will discuss the transfer of property in Chapter 6.

Some parcels of land are registered under the Torrens system. If you find a *Certificate of Title*, then the decedent's property is registered property. The Certificate of Title is a document filed with the Registrar of Titles in the county where the property is located. It identifies the legal description of the property and the owner(s) of the property as of the decedent's date of death (MN 508.34).

Many people keep their deeds, Abstracts or Certificates of Title in a safe deposit box. If you cannot find any of these documents in the decedent's home, then you need to determine whether he had a safe deposit box; and if so, you will need to examine the contents of the box. Access to the safe deposit box is discussed at the end of this chapter.

THE LOST DEED

If you know that the decedent owned real property (lot, residence or condominium.) but you cannot locate the deed, then contact the County Recorder in the county where the property is located. The County Recorder also serves as the Registrar of Titles. He can provide you with a certified copy of last recorded deed or a copy of the Certificate of Title (MN 508.30, 508.68, 508A.85).

You need to locate the deed to any out of state property owned by the decedent. It is the practice in some states to insure title to the property, so you may find a Title Insurance policy together with the deed. The new owner can turn in that policy and receive a discount toward the purchase new title insurance; so it is important to keep the policy together with the deed.

THE LOST OUT OF STATE DEED

If you know the decedent owned out of state real property, and cannot find the deed, you can use the same procedure just described, namely, you can check with the recording department in the county where the property is located. In some states the Clerk of the Circuit Court or Registrar of Deeds is in charge of the recording department. Most states do not issue Certificates of Title. However you can get a copy of the last recorded deed.

If you do not know where the property is located, you can wait for the next tax bill. In many states the tax bill contains its legal description, or tax identification number.

Many states index the property by the name of the owner, so if you know the county where the property is located, you should be able to find the deed by giving the decedent's name to the Clerk.

FILING THE WILL

Minnesota law requires that whoever has the original Will must deposit it with the Probate Court as soon as that person learns of the death and is asked by an interested person to deposit it with the Court. If the decedent was a resident of Minnesota, the Will should be deposited in the Probate Court in the county of his residence. If he was not a resident of Minnesota, his Will may be deposited in any county where the decedent's property is located (MN 524.2-516, 524.4-204).

The Clerk will accept an original Will only and not a copy, so it is important to hand carry the original document to the Clerk. If you are the Executor of the Will, you can give it to your attorney to file with the court as part of the Probate proceeding. Make a copy of the Will for your own records before delivering it to the Probate Court or to your attorney.

 Special Situation WILL DRAFTED IN ANOTHER STATE OR COUNTRY

A Will that conforms to the laws of the state or country where it was prepared can be admitted to Probate the same as any Will drafted in conformance with the laws of Minnesota (MN 524.2-506). A Will drafted in another language must be translated into English before it can be admitted into Probate.

A Will that has been admitted to Probate in another state can be used to distribute property here in Minnesota, provided the Personal Representative provides the Probate Court with an authentic copy of the Will (MN 524.3-301).

**☎ LAWYER**

OUT OF STATE RESIDENCE OR PROPERTY

If the decedent had his residence in Minnesota and owned property in another state, you may need to have an initial Probate proceeding in Minnesota and an *ancillary* (secondary) proceeding in the other state. If the decedent had his residence in another state and owned property in Minnesota, then it may need to be done the other way around; namely, you may need to conduct the initial Probate in the other state and the ancillary Probate proceeding in Minnesota.

Minnesota law allows the initial Probate proceeding for an out of state resident to be conducted in Minnesota whenever the decedent owns property located within this state. Other states have similar laws, namely if the decedent was a resident of Minnesota, they will allow the initial Probate proceeding to be conducted in the county where the decedent's property is located.

If you are going to be Personal Representative, and the decedent owned property in another state or was a resident of another state, you should consult with an experienced Probate attorney in each state to determine where the initial Probate should be conducted. Convenience is an important consideration, but you also need to consider that each state has its own tax structure and Probate statutes. Ask each attorney whether the location of the initial Probate proceeding will have any effect on the total cost of the Probate proceeding, who is to inherit the property or how much the Estate will be taxed.

THE MISSING WILL

People tend to put off making a Will until they think they need to. For many, that need arises when they are elderly and/or seriously ill and have assets that they want to leave to someone. Young people with few assets usually do not have a Will. People who are aged and with significant assets usually have a Will or Trust.

A survey conducted for the American Association of Retired Persons ("AARP") found that the probability of having a Will increases with age. Forty-four percent of those surveyed who were between the ages of 50 to 54 had a Will. This increased to 85% for those who were 80 and older. You can find more details of the survey at their Web site:

   AARP WEB SITE
http://research.aarp.org

Those who make a Will, usually tell the person that they appoint as Executor, of the existence of the Will. Chances are, that someone in the decedent's circle of family and friends, knows whether there is a Will.

If you believe that the decedent had a Will, but you cannot find it, then there are at least three places to check out:

⇨   **THE CLERK OF THE PROBATE COURT**
Minnesota law gives residents the right to deposit their Will with the Clerk of the Probate Court, so the decedent could have deposited his Will with the Clerk prior to his death. Check with the Clerk in any city or county where the decedent lived. If the Will is on file, the Clerk can admit the Will to Probate. If Probate is to be conducted in another Court, the Clerk will deliver the Will to that Court (MN 524.2-515).

⇨ THE DECEDENT'S ATTORNEY

Look at the decedent's checkbook for the past few years and see whether he paid any attorney fees. If you are able to locate the decedent's attorney, then call and inquire whether the attorney ever drafted a Will for the decedent, and if so, whether the attorney has the original Will in his possession. If the attorney has the original Will, then ask the attorney to forward the Will to the Probate court. Asking the attorney to forward the Will to the court does not obligate you to employ the attorney should you later find that a Probate proceeding is necessary.

⇨ THE SAFE DEPOSIT BOX

Many people keep their original Will in a safe deposit box. If you believe that the decedent had a Will but you cannot find it, then check to see if the decedent had a safe deposit box. If he did, you will need to gain entry to that box to see whether the Will is in the box. See the next page for an explanation of how to gain entry to the safe deposit box.

 **☎ LAWYER**   A COPY BUT NO ORIGINAL

In Minnesota, a person can revoke his Will simply by destroying it (burning, tearing, etc.) (MN 524.2-507). If you have a copy of the Will and cannot find the original, you can ask the Judge to accept the copy into Probate, but if anyone objects, a *Formal Probate* procedue will be necessary. A Formal Probate proceeding is held when there is any contested Probate matter. The Court will resolve the issue after conducting a hearing and examining all the evidence. (MN 524.3-401, 524.3-402). Before offering a copy of the Will, it is important to consult with an attorney who is experienced in contested Probate matters.

ACCESSING THE SAFE DEPOSIT BOX

If the decedent leased a safe deposit box together with another person, each with free access to the box, the surviving joint renter of the box is free to go to the box and remove any or all of the contents of the box. If the decedent leased the box in his name only, and he gave someone (his deputy or agent) authority to access the box during his lifetime, the safe deposit box company will not allow that deputy or agent to access the box once the company is notified of the death. There are different types of companies licensed to lease safe deposit boxes in Minnesota. For simplicity we will refer to such lessor as the "bank."

If the decedent rented a safe deposit box in his name only, and a Probate proceeding is necessary, then once the Personal Representative has received his Letters, he can get access to the box and remove all of its contents. But it may happen that the original Will is in the safe deposit box. The person named as Personal Representative will need to produce the original Will before he can receive his Letters. In such case, he can give the bank an *Affidavit* (a sworn written statement) saying that he needs to search the box for the original Will.

It could happen that the decedent leased a safe deposit box in his name only and no one knows whether the decedent had a Will. In such case, his spouse or a beneficiary of the decedent's Estate or the person who was his deputy or agent, can give the bank an Affidavit stating that they wish to enter the box to conduct a Will search and/or take an inventory of the contents of the box (MN 55.10). Banks usually have an Affidavit available for such occasion; however, there is a sample Affidavit on the opposite page that you can take with you to the bank just in case they do not have one.

AFFIDAVIT PURSUANT TO MINNESOTA STATUTE 55.10

State of Minnesota

County of _____

_____ , the Affiant, first being duly sworn on oath, deposes and say that:

1. Affiant resides at

_____

in the State of _____ that his business is that of

_____

2. The decedent _____ died on _____
   A certified copy of the death certificate is attached as Exhibit A.

3. The decedent was a lessee of a safe deposit box located at
   _____ (name,address of bank)

4. Affiant's relation to the decedent is _____; and
   Affiant's is an interested person as defined by statute 55.10.

4. Affiant wishes to open the box for one or more of the following purposes:
   (i)   a will search;
   (ii) to obtain a document required to facilitate the lessee's wishes regarding body, funeral, or burial arrangements;
   (iii) to obtain an inventory of the contents of the box.

5. To the best of Affiant's knowledge and belief:
(a) no one has been appointed as Personal Representative of the decedent's Estate and
(b) no one has voiced an objection to the search of the box.

_____
Affiant

Subscribed and sworn to before me on this day _____

_____
Notary Public

Statute 55.10 requires that a company employee be present when the safe deposit box is opened. If you need to enter the box, you should call the bank and make an appointment to meet with an officer of the bank. You may want to ask if there is a charge to enter the safe deposit box; and what document or identification they require. Most banks require a certified copy of the death certificate.

Under Minnesota law, the bank is not required to allow access to the box. They can refuse entry to anyone who does not have the key or comination to the safe deposit box. They will refuse entry if anyone has voiced an objection to the search, or if they have been notified that a Personal Representative has been appointed.

If the Will is found in the box, the employee will make a copy of the document, place the copy into the box, and send the original document to the Clerk of the Court in the county where the decedent lived. If the decedent was not a resident of Minnesota, the employee will forward the Will to the Court in the county where the bank is located. Any deed to a burial lot or any document that contains instructions for the decedent's burial may be copied by the employee and given to the interested person requesting entry to the safe deposit box. If the interested person requests an inventory of the contents of the box, the employee will do so, give a copy of the inventory to the interested person and deliver the original inventory to the Clerk of the Probate Court (MN 55.10).

The rest of the items in the safe deposit box will be removed by the Personal Representative as soon as he receives his Letters. If no Probate proceeding is necessary and the contents of the safe deposit box do not exceed $20,000 the beneficiary of the decedent's Estate can get possession of those items by using the Affidavit on page 140 of this book.

What Bills Need To Be Paid? 4

The Personal Representative has the duty to be sure that all valid *claims against the Estate* (demand for payment) are paid. If the decedent had debts, but no money or property, then of course, there is no way to pay the claim. The only remaining question is whether anyone else is responsible to pay the decedent's debts. If the decedent was married, then the first person the creditor will look to, is the decedent's spouse. To understand the basis of this expectation, you need to know a bit of the history of our legal system.

Our laws are derived from English Common Law. Under early English Common Law, a single woman had the right to own property in her own name and also the right to contract to buy or sell property; but when she married, her legal identity merged with her spouse. She could not hold property free from her husband's claim or control. She could no longer enter into a contract without her husband's permission.

Once married, a woman became financially dependent on her husband. He, in turn, became legally responsible to provide his wife with basic necessities — food, clothing, shelter. If anyone provided basic necessities to his wife, then regardless of whether the husband agreed to be responsible for the debt, he became obliged to pay for them. This law was called the DOCTRINE OF NECESSARIES.

States in America departed from English Common Law by enacting a series of Married Women's Rights Acts giving a married woman the right to own property and to contract in her own name (MN 519.01, 519.02).

After these laws were passed, cases followed that tested whether the Doctrine of Necessaries still applied. Judges had to decide:

If a wife can own property and contract to pay for her own necessaries, should her husband be responsible for her debts, in the event that she does not have enough money to pay for them?

For those states deciding to continue to hold the husband liable, a second question to be decided was:

If the husband is responsible for his wife's necessaries, should she be responsible for his?

In some states, notably Florida, courts decided that neither partner was responsible to pay the other's necessities, unless they contracted or agreed to do so.

Minnesota took the opposite position. Minnesota statute 519.05 requires that if a husband and wife are living together, they are ***jointly and severally liable*** to pay for all necessary household item and supplies furnished to and used by the family; meaning that both partners together are responsible to pay for the family's necessaries and each partner, individually, is liable to pay for the family's necessaries. In fact, the statute was changed in the year 2001 to include payment for necessary medical services furnished to the family.

This law does not mean that each spouse is responsible for all of the debts of his partner. If a spouse owes a business debt, or owes money for a non-necessary item used for his/her own benefit, then the spouse is not responsible to pay that debt unless the spouse agreed to do so.

JOINT DEBTS

A *joint debt* is a debt that two or more people are responsible to pay. Usually the contract or promissory note states that the parties agree to joint and several liability. A joint debt can also be in the form of monies owed by one person with payment guaranteed by another person. If the person who owes the money does not pay, then the *guarantor* (the person who guaranteed payment) is responsible to make payment. If the decedent was single, his hospital bills, nursing home bills, funeral expenses, legal fees incurred because of the decedent's death are all debts of the decedent's Estate. They are not joint debts unless someone guaranteed payment for monies owed.

SPOUSAL DEBTS

Loans signed by the decedent and his spouse are joint debts, as are charges on credit cards that both were authorized to use. Property taxes are a joint debt if the decedent and the spouse both owned the property. And as explained, the surviving spouse is liable for all monies owed by the decedent for necessaries, including medical bills.

PAYING FOR THE JOINT DEBT

Under Minnesota law, if the decedent was liable to pay a joint debt, or if there is a judgment to pay that joint debt, and there are sufficient funds in the decedent's Estate, then the Estate is responsible to pay the entire debt. Of course, if paying the debt results in the unjust enrichment of one of the beneficiaries of the decedent's Estate, the matter can be brought before the Probate Court for a determination of the rights of the parties (MN 524.3-817).

JOINT PROPERTY BUT NO JOINT DEBT

Suppose all of the decedent's funds are held jointly with his spouse or a family member and the joint owner of the account is not responsible to pay the debt. Can the creditor require that account funds be set aside to pay the debt? If there is not enough money in the decedent's Probate Estate to pay all his debts, taxes and cost of administration the answer to the question is "Yes." It doesn't make any difference whether the account is held by a husband and wife, or whether the account is held jointly by the decedent and another. The creditor can make a claim on all of the money in the joint account. It will be up to the surviving joint owner to protect his share of the account by proving which portion of the joint account belonged to the surviving owner and not to the decedent.

A creditor has two years to come forward and demand payment from the decedent's share of the account. The time period can be shortened if there is a Probate proceeding. Once a Personal Representative is appointed the Court Administrator will publish notice in a legal newspaper notifying creditors that they have 4 months to present their claims. If there is not enough money in the Probate Estate to pay a valid claim, the creditor can demand that the Personal Representative take legal action to get possession of any account that was in the decedent's name on the date of his death (MN 524.3-801, 524.6-207).

If no Probate proceeding is necessary and you have inherited the decedent's property either through joint ownership or perhaps as a named beneficiary of an account, you can take possession of the monies in the account, but you need to keep in mind that any unpaid creditor has up to two years to take legal action to recover the decedent's share of that account.

NO MONEY — NO PROPERTY

If the decedent owed money then the debt needs to be paid from assets owned by the decedent — which leads to the next question "Did the decedent have any money in his own name when he died?"

If the decedent died without any money or property in his name, then there is no money to pay any creditor. The only question that remains is whether anyone else is liable to pay those bills. The issue of payment most often arises in relation to services provided by nursing homes. When a person enters a nursing home, he is usually too ill to speak for himself or even sign his name. In such cases, the nursing home administrator will ask the spouse or a family member to sign a battery of papers on behalf of the patient before allowing the patient to enter the facility. Buried in that battery of papers may be a statement that the family member agrees to be responsible for payment to the nursing home. As explained, in Minnesota the spouse is required to be responsible for all nursing home bills regardless of whether the spouse agrees to be liable; however if the patient is single and no family member agrees to be responsible to pay for the patient's car, the facility may refuse to admit the patient.

If a nursing home accepts Medicare or Minnesota Medical Assistance (Medicaid) payments, then, under the Federal Nursing Home Reform Law, the nursing home is prohibited from requiring a family member to guarantee payment as a condition of allowing the patient to enter that facility (USC Title 42 §1395I-3(c)(5)(A)(ii)). Nonetheless, some nursing home administrators, in effect, will say "Either someone agrees to pay for the patient's bill or you need to find a different facility."

Their position is understandable. Most nursing homes are business establishments and not charitable organizations. The nursing home must be paid for the services they provide or they soon will be out of business. For an insolvent patient, the solution to the problem is to have the patient admitted to a facility and immediately apply for Medical Assistance.

But suppose the decedent had some money when he entered the nursing home and you agreed to guarantee payment to the nursing home?

What if you feel that you were coerced into signing as a guarantor?

Are you now liable to pay the decedent's final nursing home bill if your family member died without funds?

An experienced Elder Law attorney will be able to answer these questions after examining the documents that you signed and the conditions under which the patient entered the nursing home.

PAYING THE DECEDENT'S BILLS

If the decedent was married and no Probate proceeding is necessary, then the surviving spouse needs to make provision for paying bills they were both responsible to pay. If the decedent was not married and he owned property belonging to him alone, such as a bank account, securities or real property, then paying monies owed by the decedent falls to the Personal Representative.

Just as soon as he is appointed, the Representative is required to make a diligent effort to locate all of the decedent's creditors and give them written notice that they have 30 days from receipt of that notice to file a claim against the Estate (MN 524.3-801).

The Personal Representative needs to look over each claim and decide whether that claim is valid. The problem with making that decision is that the decedent is not here to say whether he actually received the goods and services that are now being billed to his Estate.

That is especially the case for medical or nursing care bills. An example of improper billing brought to the attention of this author was that of a bill submitted for a physical examination of the decedent. The bill listed the date of the examination as July 10th, but the decedent died on July 9th. Other incorrect billings may not be as obvious, so each invoice needs to be carefully examined.

If the Personal Representative decides to challenge a bill, and is unable to settle the matter with the creditor, then the Probate court will decide whether the debt is valid and should be paid.

MEDICAL BILLS COVERED BY INSURANCE

If the decedent had health insurance you may receive an invoice stamped "THIS IS NOT A BILL." This means the health care provider has submitted the bill to the decedent's health insurance company and expects to be paid by them. Even though payment is not requested, it is important to verify that the bill is valid for two reasons:

➢ **LATER LIABILITY**

If the insurer refuses to pay the claim, the facility will seek payment from whoever is in possession of the decedent's property, and that may reduce the amount inherited by the beneficiaries.

➢ **INCREASED HEALTH CARE COSTS**

Regardless of whether the decedent was covered by a private health care insurer or Medicare, improper billing increases the cost of health insurance to all of us. Consumers pay high premiums for health coverage. We, as taxpayers, all share the cost of Medicare. If unnecessary or fraudulent billing is not checked, then ultimately, we all pay.

 **MEDICARE FRAUD**

Special Situation

If you believe that you have come across a case of Medicare fraud, you can call the ANTI-FRAUD HOTLINE (800)447-8477 and report the incident to the Office of the Inspector General of the United States Department of Health and Human Services.

HOW TO CHECK MEDICARE BILLING

If the decedent was covered by Medicare, then an important billing question is whether the health care provider agreed to accept Medicare *assignment of benefits*, meaning that they agreed to accept payment directly from Medicare. If so, the maximum liability for the patient is **20%** of the amount determined as reasonable by Medicare. For example, suppose a doctor bills Medicare $1,000 for medical treatment of the decedent. If Medicare determines that a reasonable fee is $800, then the patient is liable for 20% of the $800 ($160).

Health care providers who do not accept Medicare assignment bill the patient directly. They can charge up to 15% more than the amount allowed by Medicare. If the decedent knew and agreed to be liable for the payment, then his Estate may be liable for whatever Medicare doesn't pay. For example, if a doctor's bill is $1,000 and Medicare allows $800, then Medicare will reimburse the decedent's Estate 80% of $800 ($640). The doctor may charge the Estate 15% more than the $800 ($920) and the Estate may be liable for the difference: $920 - $640 or $280.

To summarize:
For health care providers accepting Medicare assignment, the most they can bill the decedent's Estate is 20% of what Medicare allows (not 20% of what they bill.)

Those who do not accept Medicare assignment, can bill 15% more than the amount allowed by Medicare. The decedent's Estate may be liable for the difference between the amount billed and the amount paid by Medicare.

In either case, if the decedent had secondary health care insurance, then the secondary insurer may be responsible to pay for the difference.

If the health care provider reports to you that a service provided to the decedent is not covered by Medicare, or if the facility submits the bill to Medicare and Medicare refuses to pay, then check to see if you agree with that ruling by determining what services are covered under Medicare. See page 45 of this book for information about how to obtain a pamphlet that explains what medical treatments are covered under Medicare. If you have specific billing questions about Part A, you can call Blue Cross Blue Shield of Minnesota at (800) 655-1636. For Part B questions call Trailblazer Health Enterprises (800) 444-4606. For the hearing impaired call TTY/TDD (877) 486-2048.

APPEALING THE DECISION

If you believe that the decedent was wrongly denied coverage, then you can appeal that decision. The State Health Insurance Program ("SHIP") can explain how to go about filing a Medicare appeal. You can call the Minnesota Department of Aging at (800) 243-3425 for a referral to the SHIP office nearest you.

If you want an attorney to assist with your appeal, call the Minnesota Bar at (800) 492-1964 for a referral to an attorney experienced in Medicare appeals. Some attorneys work **pro bono** (literally for the public good; i.e. without charge) but most charge to assist in an appeal. Federal statute 42 U.S.C. §406(a)(2)(A) limits the amount an attorney may charge for a successful Medicare appeal to 25% of the amount recovered or $4,000, whichever is the smaller amount.

THE MEDICAL ASSISTANCE CLAIM

Medicaid, which is known as *Medical Assistance*, in Minnesota is a program that provides medical and long term nursing care for people with low income and limited resources. The program is funded jointly by the federal and state government. Federal law requires the state to recover monies spent from the Estate of a Medical Assistance recipient who received assistance when he was 55 or older. The state will seek reimbursement for the cost of nursing home care and other home or community based services. Both state and federal law prohibit any recovery of monies spent, until the surviving spouse, and/or disabled child of the decedent are deceased (MN 256B.15, 42 U.S.C. 1396(p).

Usually there is no money to recover because to qualify the applicant must have limited income and few assets, however if the decedent was married, the state will wait until the death of the surviving spouse and then seek recovery from the Estate of the surviving spouse. For example, suppose the decedent owned his homestead jointly with his spouse. Owning the homestead with a spouse, does not disqualify a person from receiving Medicaid benefits; but once the spouse dies, the state will make a claim against the homestead for monies spent on the Medicaid recipient. Even if the homestead was in the spouse's name only, the state still has a right to place a claim on the Estate of the surviving spouse for monies spent on the decedent, because, under Minnesota law married couples are each responsible to pay for the necessaries of the other and that includes payments for medical and nursing care (MN 519.05).

To summarize: Monies spent by the state on the care of the decedent are a debt to decedent's Estate AND to the Estate of the surviving spouse.

SPOUSE DIES BEFORE MEDICAID RECIPIENT

It often happens that the Medical Assistance recipient is the surviving spouse. If the spouse of the Medicaid recipient dies, and there are no minor or disabled children, the county or local administrative agency for Medical Assistance will file a claim on the spouse's Estate for monies spent on behalf of the Medicaid recipient (MN 524.2-215).

In addition, the county has the right to demand that the Medicaid recipient receive as much of the spouse's Estate as allowed under Minnesota law. We will discuss how much the surviving spouse is entitled to inherit in Chapter 5.

If the amount inherited by the Medical Assistance recipient exceeds the amount spent by the state, then the recipient will be responsible to pay for his own care until those funds are spent.

There are exceptions to these rules. The state will not require the Medical Assistance recipient to enforce his right to inherit property from the spouse if the couple signed a valid prenuptial agreement in which the Medical Assistance recipient waived (gave up) his right to inherit property from his spouse. And the county will not pursue the claim if to do so will cause undue hardship. But undue hardship is not easily proven. It will take the efforts of an experienced Elder Law attorney to present the facts to the state.

If you have a question about Medical Assistance recoveries, or you need a referral to Legal Services, you can call the Senior LinkAge Line at (800) 333-2433.

SOME THINGS ARE CREDITOR PROOF

Sometimes it happens that the decedent had money or property titled in his name only, but he also had a significant amount of debt. In such cases the beneficiaries may wonder whether they should go through a Probate proceeding if there will be little, if anything, left after the creditors are paid. Before making the decision consider that some assets are protected under Minnesota law:

✧ ACCIDENT/DISABILITY PROCEEDS ✧

Monies paid to a beneficiary as proceeds of an accident or disability insurance on the decedent are free from the claims of the decedent's creditors. The proceeds are even free from claims of the beneficiary's creditors (MN 550.39).

✧ EXEMPTIONS FOR SURVIVING SPOUSE ✧

Minnesota law allows the decedent's surviving spouse and/or child to inherit certain items free from the claims of creditors.

LIFE INSURANCE PROCEEDS

The decedent's spouse and/or child can receive up to $20,000 of the proceeds of a life insurance free from the claims of his creditors. The $20,000 can be increased by $5,000 for each dependent of the surviving spouse or child. For example, if the decedent's child has 3 dependents, say his wife and two children, then the child can inherit up to $35,000 of insurance proceeds free from the claims of his deceased parent (MN 550.37).

✧ EMPLOYEE BENEFITS

Plans governed by the Employee Retirement Income Security Act ("ERISA") are creditor proof, as are monies paid as a Veteran's pension or other benefits by the federal or state government. Annuities, pensions, profit sharing or other retirement plans, including IRA's and Keogh accounts are creditor proof up to a present value of $30,000 and additional amounts to the extent that such funds are reasonably necessary for the support of the surviving spouse or dependents (MN 550.37, 550.38, 29 U.S.C. sec. 1001, et seq.).

In general, income taxes have not been paid from these funds, so If you inherit money from the decedent's pension, annuity or retirement allowance, you should consult with an attorney or an accountant to determine how much money needs to be set aside to pay for federal and state income taxes.

✧ EXEMPT PROPERTY

The surviving spouse is entitled to keep the decedent's:

⇨ personal effects, furniture, and furnishings up to a maximum value of $10,000 and

⇨ automobile no matter what its value.

If there is no surviving spouse, then the decedent's children are entitled to share these items equally between them. Any child who was intentionally omitted from the decedent's Will is not entitled to any share of the Exempt Property (MN 524.2-403).

✧ THE HOMESTEAD

Each homeowner in the state of Minnesota is allowed to keep up to $200,000 of the value of his homestead free from creditor's claims. For those homesteads that are used primarily for agricultural purpose, $500,000 of the homestead value is exempt from creditors. There is only one homestead exemption for a married couple. The exemption extends to the creditors of the husband and/or the wife regardless of whether the homestead is titled in the husband's name or the wife's name or in both their names.

If the homestead was in the decedent's name only, and it is inherited by the decedent's spouse or descendants, it is exempt from all debts, that were not valid charges on the property at the time of his death. Valid charges on the property would include:

— Liens Placed Prior To Death

Any mortgage on the property remains in effect. Payments need to continue to be paid or the lender can foreclose against the property. Similarly, tax liens, mechanics liens, and any lien on the property because of a judgment against the decedent, remains in effect.

— Public Assistance Liens

Medical Assistance liens as discussed on the prior page remain in effect. Once the surviving spouse is deceased, the Minnesota Department of Social Services can place a lien against the Estate for recovery of monies spent on behalf of either the wife or husband or both.

The homestead is inherited by the surviving spouse or descendants free from the costs of administration, funeral bills, and any claim (other than the above liens) filed after his death (MN 510.01, 510.04, 510.05, 510.06, 524.2-402).

✧ THE FAMILY ALLOWANCE

The following family members are entitled to a Family Allowance for their reasonable support during the Probate proceeding:

⇨ the surviving spouse

⇨ the decedent's minor children who
he was obliged to support

⇨ any child who was being supported by the decedent.

The Personal Representative determines how much Family Allowance to award, provided the amount is not greater than $1,500 per month. He will pay the Allowance to the surviving spouse; or to whoever has care of the children in the event spouse is deceased. If there is not enough money in the Estate to pay all claims against the Estate, then the Family Allowance cannot be awarded for more than a year. If there are sufficient funds to pay all claims, then the Family allowance can be paid up to 18 months (MN 524.2-404).

✧ THERE IS A PRIORITY OF PAYMENT ✧

Next, consider that not all Probate debts are equal. If there are insufficient funds in the Probate Estate to pay for all claims against the decedent's Estate, then Minnesota statute establishes an order of priority for payment:

CLASS 1: COSTS AND EXPENSES OF ADMINISTRATION

Top priority is any cost or expense associated with the administration of the Estate. This includes filing fees, accounting and appraisal fees, Personal Representative and attorney fees.

CLASS 2: FUNERAL EXPENSES

Reasonable funeral expenses are second in line for payment.

CLASS 3: FEDERAL TAXES

Debts and taxes owed by the decedent (or his Estate) to the federal government are a class 3 debt.

CLASS 4: EXPENSES OF LAST ILLNESS

Fourth in line for payment are the reasonable and necessary medical and nursing care costs of the decedent's last illness. This includes payment made to those who were caring for the decedent prior to his death. It also includes claims filed by the Minnesota Department of Social Services for repayment of Medical Assistance given to the decedent.

CLASS 5: MEDICAL EXPENSES FOR LAST YEAR OF LIFE

Any reasonable and necessary medical, hospital or nursing home expense for the care of the decedent during his last year of life is a class 5 debt.

CLASS 6: STATE TAXES

Taxes, and penalties owed by the decedent to the state of Minnesota are a class 5 debt.

CLASS 7: ALL OTHER CLAIMS

No payment can be made to a given class until monies owed to those in a prior class are paid. And there is no preference of payment within a given class with the exception of class 4. Any monies spent by the decedent or by his relatives for his care during his last illness has priority over the claim of the state for reimbursement of public assistance funds.

If there is not enough money to pay everyone in any other class, then whatever money is available is divided proportionally between them; with the exception of the Class 4 claims as above described (MN 246.53, 524.3-805).

✧ THERE IS A STATUTE OF LIMITATIONS ✧

There are federal and state laws that set time periods for pursuing a claim. Anyone who wishes to take court action must do so within the time period set by the given Statute of Limitation. For example, in Minnesota, a suit for wages or overtime must be filed within 3 years. The Personal Representative does not need to pay any claim against the decedent's Estate if the Statute of Limitations period passed before his death. If the time limit has not passed, then the Statute of Limitations is suspended for 12 months following the date of death. Even though the Statute of Limitations is suspended, whoever wishes to pursue the claim against the decedent's Estate must do so within the Statute of Limitations for filing a claim.

Once a Personal Representative is appointed, the Court Administrator will publish a notice once a week for 2 weeks in a legal newspaper in the county where the Probate proceeding is being conducted. Creditors have 4 months from the first date of publication to file their claim. If any creditor is known to the Personal Representative, he must send a copy of the notice to that creditor. The creditor then has 30 days from the day he received the notice or 4 months after notice was first published in the newspaper. No claim can be pursued unless it is filed within the given time period (MN 524.3-801, 524.3-802, 524.3-803, 541.07).

But what if no one starts a Probate proceeding?
Under Minnesota statute, a claim that not filed within 1 year after the death, cannot be enforced against the Estate, the Personal Representative, or any of the beneficiaries. There are exceptions to the one-year limit such as mortgages and federal claims and certain liens on the decedent's property. But, in general, if no one begins a Probate proceeding until one year has passed, then the beneficiaries may be able to obtain possession of the decedent's assets free from creditor claims.

Guiding Those Left Behind In Minnesota

 **LAWYER**

DECEDENT LEAVING CONSIDERABLE DEBT

If the decedent died leaving much debt and no property, then the solution is simple. No Probate, no one gets paid. But if the decedent had property and died owing more money than the property was worth, his heirs may decide to just not bother starting a Probate proceeding, or maybe just wait out the year.

This may not be the best decision. Some creditors are tenacious and will use whatever legal strategy is available in order to be paid, including initiating the Probate proceeding themselves. If no one starts a Probate proceeding, then after 45 days from the date of death, a creditor can petition (ask) the court to be appointed as Personal Representative of the Estate.

If the creditor is appointed, he can determine whether anyone benefited because of the death as a joint owner of the decedent's real or personal property or through any other non-probate transfer. As Personal Representative, the creditor would have the legal right to require such beneficiary to contribute as much of the inheritance as is necessary to pay any valid claim against the decedent's Estate (MN 524.3-203, 524.3-901, 524.6-204, 573.09).

Before you decide to distance yourself from the Probate proceeding, or wait out the year, consult with an attorney experienced in Probate matters, for an his opinion about the best way to administer the Estate.

MONIES OWED TO THE DECEDENT

Suppose you owed money to the decedent. Do you need to pay that debt now that he is dead? That depends on whether there is some written document that says the debt is forgiven once the decedent dies. For example, suppose the decedent lent you money to buy your home. If he left a Will saying that once he dies, your debt is forgiven, then you do not need to make any more payments. If you signed a promissory note and mortgage at the time you borrowed the money from the decedent, then the Personal Representative should sign the original promissory note "**PAID IN FULL**" and return the note to you. If the mortgage was recorded, then the Personal Representative should sign and record a satisfaction of mortgage with the County Recorder in the county where the property is located. You should receive the recorded satisfaction of mortgage as proof of payment of the debt.

If you owed the decedent money and there is no Will, or if there is a Will, no mention of forgiving the debt, then you still owe the money. Monies borrowed from the decedent and his spouse need to be repaid to the spouse. Monies borrowed from the decedent only, become an asset to the Estate of the decedent, meaning that you owe the money to the decedent's Estate. If you are one of the beneficiaries of the Estate, you can deduct the money from your inheritance.

For example, suppose your father left $70,000 in a bank account to be divided equally between you and your two brothers. If you owed your father $20,000, then your father's Estate is really worth $90,000. Instead of paying the $20,000, you can agree to receive $10,000 and have the $20,000 debt forgiven. Each of your brothers will then receive $30,000 in cash.

Who Are The Beneficiaries? 5

A question that comes up early on is who is entitled to the property of the decedent. To answer the question you first need to know how the property was titled (owned) as of the date of death.

There are three ways to own property. The decedent could have owned property jointly with another person; or in trust for another person; or the decedent could have owned property that was titled in his name only.

In general, upon the decedent's death:

Joint Property belongs to the surviving joint owner.

Trust Property belongs to the beneficiary
of the Trust.

Property owned by the **decedent only** is inherited
by the beneficiaries named in the Will.
If there is no Will, then the property goes to his heirs
according to Minnesota's Laws of Intestate Succession.

NOTE ⇨ If the decedent was married, then his
spouse may have rights in his property.

This chapter describes each type of ownership in detail.

PROPERTY HELD JOINTLY

Bank accounts, securities, motor vehicles, real property can all be owned jointly by two or more people. If one of the joint owners dies, the surviving owners continue to own their share of the property. Who owns the share belonging to the decedent depends on how the joint ownership was set up:

THE JOINT BANK ACCOUNT

If a bank account is opened in two or more names, then each depositor is given a statement of the terms and conditions of the account. The statement will say whether each depositor has authority to make a withdrawal, or whether two signatures are necessary.

Each owner of a joint account owns as much of the account as was contributed by that person to the account. Unless the account states differently, in Minnesota, a joint account is a survivorship account. Should one of the joint owners die, his share goes to the surviving owner. If there are two or more surviving owners, the decedent's share is divided equally between them (MN 524.6-201, 524.6-203, 524.6-204).

Of course, any of the surviving owners can go to the bank and withdraw all of the funds in the account (MN 524.6-209). With such an arrangement, the surviving owners need to cooperate with each other to divide the funds equitably between them. And the surviving owners need to keep in mind that for 2 years after the death, any of the decedent's creditors can demand that the decedent's share of the account be used to pay an outstanding debt (see Page 81).

JOINTLY HELD SECURITIES

You can determine whether the decedent owns a security alone or jointly with another by examining the face of the stock or bond certificate. If two names are printed on the certificate followed by a statement that the owners are joint tenants ("JT TEN"), or joint tenants with rights of survivorship ("JTWRS")," the surviving owner can either cash in the security or ask the company to issue a new certificate in the name of the surviving owner.

A security held jointly without rights of survivorship, is held as a *Tenancy In Common.* Should one co-owner die, his share goes to whomever he named as beneficiary of his Will, or if no Will, then it goes to his heirs as determined by Minnesota's Laws of Intestate Succession (see page 115 for a discussion of the law).

Each state has its own securities regulations. If a security held in two or more names, was registered or purchased in another state, then you will need to contact the company to determine how the account was set up; i.e. with or without rights of survivorship.

If the decedent held his securities in a brokerage account, then the name of the owner of that account is printed on the monthly or quarterly brokerage statement. Not all brokerage firms print the name of a joint owner on the brokerage statement, so you need to contact the firm to determine whether there is a surviving joint owner, or perhaps a beneficiary of the account. Request a copy of the contract that is the basis of the account. The contract will show when the account was opened and the terms of the brokerage account.

JOINTLY HELD MOTOR VEHICLE

If a motor vehicle is held jointly, the name of each owner is printed on the title to the motor vehicle. Joint ownership is indicated by the words "AND" or "OR," for example, the title can read: HENRY LEE AND SUSAN LEE
or title can read: HENRY LEE OR SUSAN LEE.

Each of these designations has a different meaning.

AND The word "AND" means that both signatures are required to transfer title.

OR The word "OR" means that during the lifetime of the joint owners, either is free to transfer title on his/her signature alone.

A car that is titled as "AND" is essentially a Tenancy-In-Common The surviving owner does not automatically own the decedent's share of the car. The decedent's "half" descends in the same manner as property titled as a Tenancy-In-Common; i.e., to a named beneficiary in a Will or according to Minnesota's Laws of Intestate Succession.

Upon the death of a joint owner of a car titled as "OR" the surviving owner can go to the nearest Motor Vehicle Registrar Office and change title to the name of the surviving owner.

It is important to change title as soon as you are able. You might be able to get a reduced insurance rate if there is only one person insured under the policy. Also, should the surviving owner be involved in an accident, and title has officially been changed, then there is no question that the Estate of the decedent is in any way liable for the accident.

The name of the owner of real property is printed on the face of the deed. To determine whether the decedent owned the property jointly with another person, look at the last recorded deed or Certificate of Title. See page 72 if you cannot locate these documents.

WARRANTY DEED

ROBERT TRAYNOR, a single man, Grantor
of Clay County, Minnesota, for and in
consideration of $70,000
conveys and warrants to
ROBERT TRAYNOR, JR. a married man and
HENRY TRAYNOR, a single man, Grantee
as joint tenants
and not as tenants in common,
the following described real estate

. . .

Robert Traynor is the **Grantor** of the deed. That means he transferred the property to Robert Jr. and Henry Traynor who are the **Grantees** and present owners of the property. Should one of the joint tenants die, then the surviving joint tenant owns the property 100%. Nothing need be done to establish the ownership, however the decedent's name remains on the deed.

See Chapter 6 for a discussion about how to record documents that will notify anyone who is examining title to the property that there is just one owner.

🗏 DEED WITH A LIFE ESTATE

A *Life Estate* interest in real property means that the person who owns the Life Estate has the right to live in that property until he/she dies. You can identify a Life Estate interest by examining the face of the deed. If somewhere on the face of the deed you see the phrase RESERVING A LIFE ESTATE to the decedent, then the Grantee now owns the property. For example, suppose the granting paragraph of the deed reads:

PETER REILLY, a single man, Grantor
whose address is
123 Main Street, Rochester, MN

. . .

conveys and warrants to
to ROSE SMITH, a married woman,

. . .

RESERVING A LIFE ESTATE TO THE GRANTOR

Peter Reilly is the owner of the Life Estate. While he is alive, the Grantee (Rose Smith) has no right to occupy the property. Once Peter dies, Rose will own the property, and will be free to take possession of the property or sell or transfer it, all as she sees fit.

As with a survivorship tenancy, nothing need be done to establish Rose's ownership. Chapter 6 for a discussion of what documents need to be recorded to notify anyone who is examining title to the property that Rose is now the owner of the property.

🗏 DEED HELD AS HUSBAND AND WIFE

Real Property owned by a married couple does not have any right of survivorship, unless the deed is held by them as JOINT TENANTS. If the deed identifies them as husband and wife and does not say that they are Joint Tenants, or if they are identified as TENANTS IN COMMON, then the decedent's share belongs to whomever the decedent named as his beneficiary in his Will. If the decedent died without a Will, then the Minnesota Laws of Intestate Succession determine who inherits the decedent's share of the property (MN 500.19).

SPOUSE ▶ THE RIGHTS OF THE SPOUSE IN THE HOMESTEAD

If the decedent was survived by a spouse and no descendants, then under Minnesotal law, the homestead of the decedent goes to his surviving spouse. He can't give it away by Will or transfer it by any means, unless the spouse agrees, in writing to the transfer.

If the decedent was survived by descendants, then the surviving spouse gets a Life Estate in the homestead, and once the surviving spouse is deceased, the decedent's homestead goes to his descendents, in equal shares, *by representation*. "By representation" is explained on page 115.

If the decedent is not survived by a spouse, then the homestead goes to the beneficiaries of his Estate, in the same manner as any other item owned by the decedent (MN 524.2-402).

 DIVORCED PRIOR TO DEATH

When a couple divorce, the Decree of Dissolution usually incorporates a settlement agreement that divides the property of the couple. Under Minnesota law, unless the Decree of Dissolution states otherwise, once they are divorced, real property that they hold as Joint Tenants becomes property owned by them as Tenants In Common. If the decedent was divorced prior to his death, and the deed has not been changed, then his "half" of the property goes to the beneficiaries of his Will, or if no Will, then to his next of kin as determined by Minnesota's Laws of Intestate Succession (MN 500.19).

This law applies only to a divorced couple. If the decedent was separated from his spouse, property held by them as Joint Tenants, goes to the surviving spouse.

 THERE COULD BE A LATER DEED

The above discussion on the different types of ownership of real property assumes that you are in possession of the most recent, valid Minnesota deed. The decedent could have signed another, later, deed. Before you come to a conclusion about who inherits the property it is advisable to get a copy of the most recent deed or Certificate of Title from the County Recorder in the county where the property is located.

☎ LAWYER   OUT OF STATE DEED

The inheritance of real property located in the state of Minnesota is determined by the laws of Minnesota, and this is so regardless of whether the decedent was a resident of this state. Similarly, if the decedent owned property in another state or country, then even if the decedent was a resident of Minnesota, the laws of the state or country where the property is located determine who inherits that property.

The laws of each state are similar, but not the same. In general, property held as Joint Tenants With Rights of Survivorship belongs to the surviving joint owner, but states differ in how the deed needs to be worded in order to have a right of survivorship. In this and many other states, just the term "Joint Tenants" means that there are rights of survivorship (MN 500.19). Other states, such as Alabama, require that the deed clearly state that there are Rights Of Survivorship; and if not, the property is held as Tenants In Common.

In other states such as Florida, there is a right of survivorship whenever the deed identifies the Grantees as being married. For example, a deed that identifies the couple as "husband and wife," or a deed that identifies the couple as "Tenants-by-Entirety" is the same as a joint tenancy with right of survivorship. When one party dies, the surviving spouse owns the property 100%.

If the decedent owned property in another state, then it is important to consult with an attorney in that state to determine who now owns the property.

PROPERTY HELD IN TRUST

BANK/ SECURITY ACCOUNTS

If a bank account is registered in the name of the decedent held "in trust for" or "for the benefit of" someone, then once the bank has a certified copy of the death certificate, the bank will turn over the account to the beneficiary. If the beneficiary is not yet 18, and the amount to be transferred is not greater than $10,000 the bank can transfer the funds to an adult member of the child's family. If the amount is greater than $10,000, then no transfer can be made without permission from the Probate Court (MN 527.27). See Chapter 7 for a discussion about transferring property to a minor.

If a bank or credit union account is registered in the name of the decedent "as Trustee under a Trust agreement," that means the decedent was the Trustee of a Trust and the bank will turn over that account to the Successor Trustee of the Trust. Banks usually require a copy of the Trust agreement when the account is opened, so the bank should know the identity of the Successor Trustee.

MOTOR VEHICLE

If the motor vehicle is held in the name of the decedent "as Trustee," then the motor vehicle continues to be Trust property. The Successor Trustee will need to contact the motor vehicle bureau to have title changed to that of the Successor Trustee. If the Trust agreement directs the Successor Trustee to sell the car or to distribute that car to a beneficiary, then the Successor Trustee will do so. See Chapter 6 for a discussion of how to transfer the car.

REAL PROPERTY

If the decedent had a Trust and put real property that he owned into the Trust, then the deed may read something like this:

> JOHN ZAMORA and MARIA ZAMORA,
> his wife, whose address is
> 200 Main Street, St. Cloud, Minnesota
>
> . . .
>
> conveys and warrants to JOHN ZAMORA,
> TRUSTEE OF THE JOHN ZAMORA TRUST
> UNDER AGREEMENT
> DATED FEBRUARY 26, 2001,
> the following real property
>
> . . .

The death of the Trustee of a Trust does not change the ownership of the property. It remains in Trust. The Trust document might say whether the person who takes John's place as Trustee (the Successor Trustee) should sell or keep the property or perhaps give it to a beneficiary. If no instruction is given, the Successor Trustee can use his discretion as to what to do with the property. His decision may be affected by laws relating to the administration of Trust property in the state where the property is located.

If you are a beneficiary of the Trust and you are concerned about what the Successor Trustee will do with the property, then it is best to consult with your attorney to learn about your rights under that Trust.

PROPERTY IN DECEDENT'S NAME ONLY

If the decedent owned property that was in his name only (not jointly or in trust for someone), then some sort of Probate proceeding will be necessary before the heirs can get possession of that property. Who is entitled to the decedent's Probate Estate depends on whether the decedent died with or without a Will. If the decedent had a valid Will, then the beneficiaries of the decedent's property are identified in the Will. If the decedent died without a Will, the Minnesota Laws of Intestate Succession determine who inherits the decedent's Probate Estate and what percentage of the Probate Estate each heir is to receive once all the bills and the cost of the Probate proceeding are paid.

The law recognizes the right of the family to inherit the decedent's property. The law covers all possible relationships beginning with the decedent's spouse.

Who Is The Spouse?

In this era of people challenging the concept of the family unit, those of a philosophical bent may ponder the meaning of marriage. Is it a union of two people in the eyes of God? Is it even a union? The state does not concern itself with such things. If a person dies without a Will, then the state will distribute the decedent's Probate Estate according to the laws of the state; and the laws of the state determine whether two people are married.

MARRIED IN MINNESOTA

Minnesota legislators have defined a lawful marriage as a civil contract between a man and woman. In order to be married, each must agree to marry; obtain a marriage license and then solemnize their marriage by participating in a state or religious ceremony.

A person must be at least 16 years of age to marry in Minnesota. If a person is under 18, the parents or guardian must give their consent or the Judge of the Juvenile Court can approve the license, after investigating the facts of the case (MN 517.01, 517.02, 517.07).

Minnesota law specifically prohibits the marriage of people: ☒ who are currently married

☒ who are related closer than second cousin (MN 517.03).

THE OUT OF STATE MARRIAGE

Minnesota respects the laws of other states and countries. Marriages contracted in another state or country, and recognized as being valid in that state, are valid in the state of Minnesota — with the exception of same sex marriages (MN 517.20).

SAME SEX MARRIAGES

Vermont is the first state to recognize same sex marriages, which they refer to as a "civil union." Several states, (including Minnesota) have passed statutes that specifically deny marital status to couples of the same gender regardless of whether that marriage is valid in any other state or country.

THE COMMON LAW MARRIAGE

A common law marriage is one that has not been solemnized by ceremony. Prior to April 26, 1941, a common law marriage was valid in Minnesota, provided:

⇨ Each party was competent to enter into a marriage; meaning that they both knew what they were doing and there was no legal impediment to their union, such as being related closer than second cousin, or currently married to another; and

⇨ There was mutual consent to be married to each other; and

⇨ The couple lived together as husband and wife; and

⇨ They held themselves out as being married; meaning they told people they were married and people in the community recognized them as being married.

A common law marriage entered into in Minnesota after April 26, 1941, is not valid in the state; however courts have ruled that if the couple entered into a common law marriage in another state and that marriage was valid in that state, then Minnesota will recognize that marriage as being valid (*Laikola v. Engineered Concrete*, 277 N.W.2d, 653 (1979)).

If a marriage is valid in Minnesota, then each party has all the rights and responsibilities as provided by Minnesota law; and in particular, the right to inherit property under Minnesota's Laws of Intestate Succession.

It is important to consult with an attorney if you have any question about the validity of the decedent's marriage.

THE LAWS OF INTESTATE SUCCESSION

If the decedent died without a Will, then the state of Minnesota provides one for him in the form of the *Laws Of Intestate Succession*, which are also referred to as the *Laws of Descent and Distribution*. The decedent's *Net Probate Estate*, is what is left of the Probate Estate the funeral expenses, the cost of Probate, Homestead Allowance, Family Allowance, Exempt Property and claims are paid (MN 524.2-204). If the decedent died without a valid Will, then his Net Probate Estate is distributed as follows:

✦ MARRIED, NO CHILD OR STEPCHILD ✦

The surviving spouse inherits all of the Net Probate Estate provided the decedent had no surviving *descendant* (child, grandchild, great-grandchild, etc.) — or if all of his descendants are also descendants of the surviving spouse and his surviving spouse has no surviving descendant of her own (and not of the decedent) then the spouse inherits all of the Net Probate Estate (MN 524.2-102).

✦ CHILD, NO SPOUSE ✦

The children of an unmarried decedent inherit his Net Probate Estate in equal shares. It could happen that the decedent had a child who died before he did. The share intended for the deceased child is distributed *by representation,* which is defined by Minnesota statute 524.2-106 as follows:

> In the case of descendants of the decedent, the estate is divided into as many shares as there are surviving children of the decedent and deceased children who left descendants who survive the decedent, each surviving child receiving one share and the share of each deceased child being divided among its descendants in the same manner.

If you only had to read this definition one time to understand it, then you either are, or should be, a lawyer. For the rest of us the best way to understand this definition is by example:

ALL CHILDREN SURVIVE
Suppose the decedent was unmarried with 4 children, Ann, Barry, Carl, David and he dies intestate, then each of his children get 25% of his Estate.

CHILD WITHOUT DESCENDANTS DIES BEFORE DECEDENT
If Ann dies before her father leaving no descendants, then Barry, Carl and David divide the Estate between them and each receives one third.

CHILDREN WITH DESCENDANTS DIE BEFORE DECEDENT
Suppose instead that only Carl and David survived their father. If Ann died leaving 1 child and Barry died leaving 2 children, then the Estate is divided into 4 shares — one for each surviving child and one share for each deceased child who left descendants. Carl and David each get their 25% share. Ann's child takes her 25% share. Barry's children don't fare as well. They must divide their father's share equally between them, so each get 12 1/2%.

✧   MARRIED WITH CHILD OR STEPCHILD   ✧
The surviving spouse inherits everything provided all of the decedent's descendants are those of the spouse. If the decedent has a child of his own (not of his spouse), or if the spouse has a child not that of the decedent, the spouse is entitled to the first $150,000 and half of the balance of the Net Probate Estate. The other half descends in the same manner as if the decedent had died without a spouse or descendant; and that is explained on the next page.

✧ NO DESCENDANT, NO SPOUSE ✧

If the decedent had no spouse or descendant, then his property is divided equally between his parents. If only one of his parents is alive, then all of the property goes to that parent. If neither parent is alive, then the Net Probate Estate goes to the decedent's brothers and sisters in equal shares, by representation, i.e., if a deceased sibling has surviving descendants , then the surviving nieces and nephews take the share intended for the deceased sibling of the decedent (MN 524.2-103).

There is no distinction between full blood siblings or half blood siblings. For example, if the decedent had one brother with the same set of parents and another brother with the same father and a different mother, then both brothers inherit an equal amount (MN 524.2-107).

If there are no siblings, or any of their descendants (nieces, nephews, great nieces, great nephews, etc.), the Probate Estate is divided with half going to the decedent's maternal grandparents and half to the paternal grandparents. If only one maternal grandparent survives, then that grandparent receives half the Estate. If neither grandparent survives, then the half goes to their surviving descendants in equal shares, by representation.

If there are no descendants on the decedent's maternal side, then the entire Net Probate Estate goes to the decedent's paternal grandparents, to be distributed in the same manner as that of the maternal grandparents.

THE STATE: HEIR OF LAST RESORT

If a person dies without a Will and he has absolutely no relatives, then as a last resort, his Net Probate Estate goes to the state of Minnesota (MN 524.2-105).

CAUTION   IT ISN'T ALL THAT SIMPLE

The explanation in this book of the laws of intestate succession is abridged. Even though you may now know more about Minnesota's Laws of Intestate Succession than you ever wanted to know, there is much more to the law. For example, we did not explain in detail exactly how the Estate is distributed if the decedent is survived only by descendants of his maternal or paternal grandparents. We could give an example explaining the law, but we thought you might enjoy a puzzle instead:

Winston died intestate leaving $100,000. His only relatives were his Aunt Susie (on his mother's side) and her two children, Ramona and Abigail; and on his father's side, a second cousin, Elvis (the child of a deceased cousin). How much will each relative receive?

You can check your answer by visiting the puzzle section of the Eagle Publishing Company Web site:
http://www.eaglepublishing.com

Those who try the above puzzle will appreciate how complex Minnesota's Laws of Intestate Succession can be. Unless the descent is straight forward, with the decedent leaving a surviving spouse and/or children (all who survive him), it is best to consult with an attorney before you decide who is entitled to inherit the decedent's intestate property.

WHO INHERITS THE HOMESTEAD?

Once a person says "I do," then they each have rights in the Minnesota homestead of the other. If one of them dies, without any surviving descendant, then under Minnesota law, the decedent's homestead is inherited by the surviving spouse. The term **homestead** includes a mobile home owned and occupied by the decedent as his primary residence.

SURVIVING SPOUSE AND DESCENDANT

If the decedent has a surviving descendant, then the surviving spouse inherits a Life Estate in the property with the remainder interest going to the decedent's descendants, in equal shares, by representation.

SINGLE

A single person is free to leave his homestead to whomever he wishes. This means that if he leaves his homestead by Will, or by Trust, or by deed to a beneficiary, then that person inherits the property. If a person dies without making any provision for the inheritance of his home, his heirs will inherit the homestead according to the Minnesota Laws of Intestate Succession.

Because the surviving spouse has an ownership interest in the homestead, by law, the property cannot be given away to someone else by Will or Trust. But the right to inherit the homestead can be **waived** (given up) at any time; i.e. the parties can sign a prenuptial agreement giving up homestead rights; or after marriage either party may give up their right to the homestead by signing a document to that effect (MN 524.2-402).

THE RIGHTS OF A CHILD

ADOPTED CHILD

An adopted child has the same rights to inherit property from his adoptive parents as does a natural child. Whether the adoptive child can inherit from his natural parents depends on the circumstances of the adoption. If one of the child's parents dies, and the child is later adopted by a stepparent, then that child still has full rights of inheritance from both of his natural parents, and their respective families (MN 524.2-114).

THE AFTER BORN CHILD

Any child born to the surviving spouse within 280 days of the decedent's death has the same rights as a child who was alive at the time of death (MN 257.55).

NON-MARITAL CHILD

A child born out of wedlock has the same rights to inherit from his/her natural father as does one born in wedlock provided:

☑   after the child's birth, he and the child's biological mother married and he either acknowledged his paternity in writing, or he was required to support the child by court order, or by a voluntary written promise

— or —

☑ while the child was a minor, he received the child into his home and openly acknowledged the child as his own.

If the decedent denied his paternity, then it will take a court procedure to establish (or disprove) paternity. However there is a Statute of Limitations. No one can raise the issue in Court if the child is older than 19 years of age (MN 257.58).

THE CHILD OF AN ASSISTED CONCEPTION

Medical technology has made important contributions to solving the problem of infertility. There are all sorts of solutions, from hormone replacement therapy, to sperm banks that provide donations anonymously, to women who serve as a surrogate (gestational) mother under contract to bear a child for a couple, in many cases using the sperm or ovum of the intended parent. Solving a set of medical problems has opened the door to a new set of legal problems. Used to be, the only question was "Who's the father?" Now it could well be "Who's the mother?"

One problem addressed by the Minnesota legislature is that of artificial insemination. In this state a physician may not use artificial insemination to impregnate a married woman unless both she and her spouse give written consent. The physician is required to keep the consent on file for at least 4 years after the pregnancy is confirmed. Once the child is born, the father is listed on the birth certificate as the child's natural father (MN 257.56).

A child born to parents using artificial insemination or any other form of assisted conception, has the same rights as a child born the old fashioned way. It is presumed that the father consented to the procedure. If that is not the case, and the husband is not the father of the child, he can petition the court to terminate his parental rights and responsibilities. If the husband is successful the child will not be able to inherit from the husband, nor from his family (MN 257.57).

As of this writing, there is no specific Minnesota law addressing the issue of a child born to a surrogate mother. A child born to a surrogate mother is the child of the mother, unless adopted by the intended parents. And this is so, regardless of whether either intended parent happens to be the biological parent of the child.

WHO DIED FIRST?

Minnesota statute requires that an heir survive the decedent by at least 120 hours (5 days) in order to inherit property according to the Minnesota's Laws of Intestate Succession. If an heir does not live for at least 5 days after the decedent's death, then the decedent's property is distributed as if the heir died first. This rule also applies to the inheritance of exempt property and the homestead. The rule does not apply if it would result in the state of Minnesota inheriting property (MN 524.2-104).

Sometimes it happens that two family members die simultaneously, and no one knows who died first. For example, suppose a husband and wife die together in a car crash. In such case, each partner is assumed to have survived the other and their property distributed on that basis. For example, suppose the husband is insured, with his wife as beneficiary. The proceeds of the policy will be distributed as if the wife died before her husband. The proceeds will be given to the alternate beneficiary named in the policy. If no alternate beneficiary was named, the proceeds of the policy will go to the insured party (in this case, the husband's Estate).

Property owned jointly by the couple, with no provision for who is to inherit the property should they both die, is divided with half going to the Estate of the husband and the other half to the Estate of the wife. If they each have a Will, the husband's half is distributed according to his Will and the wife's half according to her Will. If they die intestate, then the husband's half is distributed as if he were single; and vis-versa (MN 524.2-702).

Anyone convicted of intentionally causing the death of the decedent is prohibited from profiting from the crime. Property that the killer would have inherited as a beneficiary of the decedent's Will or according to Minnesota's Laws of Intestate Succession, will be distributed as if the killer died before the decedent. Property owned jointly by the decedent and his killer becomes property held as Tenants-In-Common. This includes all real and personal property owned jointly by the decedent and his killer. The killer keeps his share, but he doesn't inherit the decedent's share. The decedent's share of the property becomes part of the decedent's Estate, to be distributed according to his Will or the Laws of Intestate Succession.

Under Minnesota law a killer may not receive the proceeds of an insurance policy on the life of the decedent. The problem with enforcing this law is that the home office of the insurance company must be notified that the beneficiary of the policy has either been convicted or accused of committing the crime. If the insurance company is notified before proceeds are distributed, the company will hold all payments until they receive a Court order directing them to make payment to whoever the Court determines is entitled to the proceeds. If the insurance company distributes the proceeds before being notified, whoever is entitled to the money will need to sue the killer in District Court — but the funds may have long since been spent (MN 524.2-803).

WHEN TO CHALLENGE THE WILL

It is not uncommon for a family member to be unhappy with the way the decedent willed his property. If you are tempted to challenge a Will, first consider whether the Will is valid under Minnesota law. In Minnesota, a Will is presumed to be valid if at the time the decedent made the Will he was at least 18 years of age and of sound mind (MN 524.2-501). Courts have ruled that a person is of sound mind if he knows how much property he has and is able to make a rational judgement. The fact that the decedent may have been old, with poor vision and even suffering from senility, does not necessarily mean he was not of sound mind when he signed the Will. It would be difficult to prove unsound mind if it was properly drafted and signed in the office of the decedent's attorney. No doubt the attorney will testify that the decedent knew exactly what he owned and was perfectly rational.

You could challenge the Will if you believe that the decedent was pressured or persuaded to sign the Will by someone close to him. To prove that he was being **unduly influenced** you will need to show that he did not act of his own free will, but rather according to the will and purpose of that person. The Court will consider many factors, such as whether the person exerting the influence had the opportunity and in fact did do so, and whether people were disinherited who would have been remembered in the Will (*In Re Estate of McQue*, 449 N.W. 2d 509 (Minn. App. 1990).

It is important to consult with an attorney experienced in Probate litigation, before you decide to challenge the Will on these or any other grounds.

THE VERBAL WILL

Picture a death bed scene. The elderly gentleman is surrounded by several family members. In a whisper, just audible enough to be heard, he says "Even though I am a wealthy man, I never got around to making a Will. You all have been good to me, but I did want my entire fortune to go to my nephew, Robert. He has been like a son to me."

Do you think Robert can inherit his Uncle's Estate?
Not in Minnesota unless:
⇨ Someone writes down his uncles's wishes, and
⇨ The uncle acknowledges that this is his Will, and
⇨ The uncle tells someone to sign the Will for him, and
⇨ The person does so, and two people sign the Will as witnesses (MN 524.2-502).
Considering that the uncle's relatives will probably inherit the fortune under the Minnesota's Laws of Intestate Succession, it is doubtful that Robert is in danger of becoming wealthy at any time in the near future.

THE UNWITNESSED WILL

You may think that the uncle would have fared better if he just sat down and wrote out a Will in his own hand when he was up to it — even if no one was present to witness his signature. Such a Will is called a *holographic Will*. Many states, including Minnesota, refuse to accept a holographic Will into Probate. The problem with a holographic Will, in this or any other state, is its authenticity. Because no one saw the decedent sign the Will, it is hard to determine whether the Will was written by the decedent or is a forgery.

THE WILL THAT IS CONTRARY TO LAW

Sometimes a person who is of sound mind, makes a Will, but that Will has the effect of giving a spouse or a minor child less than is required under Minnesota law. One such example is that of Nancy. Hers was not an easy life. She worked long hours as a waitress. She divorced her hard drinking first husband. The final judgment gave her their homestead, some securities, and sole custody of their son. After the divorce Nancy had her attorney prepare a Will leaving all she owned to her son, Richard.

Some years later she met and married Harry, a chef at the restaurant where she worked. He moved into her home and they later had twin girls. Richard was 19, and his stepsisters 12, when Nancy died after a lengthy battle with cancer.

Nancy did not leave much — her car, her home, cash and securities worth about $50,000, all of which was in her name only.

Before she died, she told Richard, that she had not changed her Will because she wanted him to have all she owned. She said Harry had a good job and she was sure he would take good care of his daughters.

No sooner was the funeral over, when Richard came in and demanded that Harry vacate his mother's home. Harry was furious and went to his attorney.

"I was a good husband to Nancy, supporting and taking care of her all during her illness. It was me, and not her son, who was at her side when she died. Now he comes in and wants to put me out of the house that I've lived in for 14 years!"

The attorney reassured him "He can't do that. Under Minnesota law you are entitled to live in that house for the rest of your life — unless you gave up your rights of inheritance by signing a prenuptial or postnuptial agreement (MN 519.11, 524.2-402). Did you sign any such document?"

"Absolutely not!"

"In that case, in addition to a life estate in your wife's home, you are allowed to keep her car and up to $10,000 in value of her personal property (furniture, furnishing, appliances, computers, jewelry, etc.) (MN 524.2-403). You and the twins are entitled up to $1,500 a month as a Family Allowance during the Probate proceeding. Assuming there is enough money in your wife's Estate to pay all of her creditors, you can receive the Family Allowance for up to 18 months. (MN 524.2-404)."

Harry was still concerned "How about the twins. Don't they have any right to inherit her Estate?"

"Yes, in fact they do. You have the right to a life estate in the homestead. Once you die it will go to the twins and your stepson in equal shares. They also have the right to inherit the same amount of their mother's Estate as their stepbrother. Under Minnesota law, if a parent makes a Will and leaves property to her child, then any child born after the Will is signed is entitled to an equal share of the property left to the child under the Will (MN 524.2-302)."

Harry said "She made that Will before we even met. Do I have the same right as the twins?

The attorney explained "You are not entitled to any share of her Estate that she left to her son, but if she willed her property to anyone else, you would have been entitled to as much of her Estate as if she died without a Will (MN 524.2-301). Not that it makes that much difference in this case. I doubt whether there will be any cash left in the Estate once the funeral expenses, medical bill, Family Allowance and the costs of Probate is paid. All that will be left is the house and the car. You get the contents of the house, the car and a life estate in the house. All Richard will get is his 1/3rd share of the house, and he won't even get that until you die or decide to move from the house."

No doubt Nancy did not understand what would happen to her Estate once she passed on. The Will she left did not accomplish her goal of providing for her son. All it did was cause an irreparable rift between Harry and Richard. It didn't need to be that way. Had Nancy known about Minnesota law, she could have consulted with an attorney and set up an Estate plan that could have provided for her son, without alienating her husband.

But, the moral of the story, for the purpose of this discussion, is that if you believe that the decedent's Will is not valid or is not drafted according to Minnesota law, then you need to consult with an attorney experienced in Probate matters to determine your legal rights under that Will.

Getting Possession Of The Property

Knowing who is entitled to receive the decedent's property is one thing. Getting that property is another. As explained in the previous chapter if the decedent held property jointly with someone, or in a trust for someone, the property now belongs to the joint owner or beneficiary. If it is personal property such as a bank account or a security, the beneficiary can usually get possession of the property by giving a certified copy of the death certificate to the financial institution.

If the decedent had real or personal property in his name only, or if he held property as a Tenant-In-Common, then some sort of Probate proceeding may be necessary in order to transfer ownership to the proper beneficiary. In most cases a full Probate proceeding is necessary and that will require the assistance of an attorney, but there are a few items that can be transferred without legal assistance. This chapter explains how to get possession of these items. The chapter also contains an explanation of the different kinds of Probate proceedings and when it is appropriate to use that procedure.

DISTRIBUTING PERSONAL PROPERTY

Too often, the first person to discover the body will help himself to the decedent's *personal effects* (clothing, jewelry, appliances, electrical equipment, cameras, books, household items and furnishing, etc.). Unless that person is the decedent's sole beneficiary, such action is unconscionable, if not illegal.

Under Minnesota law, the surviving spouse is entitled keep up to $10,000 of personal property owned by the decedent and one motor vehicle that was titled in his name, regardless of its value. If the decedent was not married, his personal property should be given to whoever is appointed as Personal Representative. The Personal Representative has the duty to distribute the property according to the decedent's Will, or if no Will, according to Minnesota law.

As explained in Chapter 4, if there is no surviving spouse, the decedent's children are entitled to these personal property items. Any child who was intentionally omitted from the decedent's Will is not entitled to take any of the decedent's personal effects; of course, if the decedent left a particular personal item to someone in his Will, the Personal Representative will distribute that item to the beneficiary of the gift (MN 524.2-403).

If there is no need for a Probate proceeding, the decedent's next of kin (as determined by the Laws of Intestate Succession) need to divide all of the personal effects among themselves in approximately equal proportions.

What's Equal?

The problem with the term "equal" is that people have different ideas of what "equal" means. Unless there is clear evidence that the decedent's Will meant something else, "equal" refers to the monetary value of the item and not to the number of items received. For example, to divide the decedent's personal property equally, one beneficiary may receive an expensive item of jewelry and another beneficiary may receive several items whose overall value is approximately equal to that single piece of jewelry.

When distributing the decedent's personal property there needs to be cooperation and perhaps compromise, or else bitter arguments might arise over items of little monetary value. One such argument occurred when an elderly woman died who was rich only in her love for her five children and nine grandchildren. After the funeral, the children gathered at their mother's apartment. Each child had his/her own furnishings and no need for anything in the apartment. They agreed to donate all of their mother's personal property to a local charity with the exception of a few items of sentimental value.

Each child took some small item as a remembrance. Things went smoothly until it came to her photograph album. Frank, the youngest sibling, said, "I'll take this." Marie objected saying, "But there are pictures in that album that I want." Frank retorted, "You already took all the pictures Mom had on her dresser." The argument went downhill from there. It almost came to blows when the eldest settled the argument: "Frank you make copies of all of the photos in the album for Marie. Marie, you make copies of all of the pictures that you took and give them to Frank. This way you both will have a complete set of Mom's pictures.

And while you're at it, make copies for the rest of us."

TRANSFERRING THE CAR

If the decedent owned a motor vehicle in his name only, then title to the car needs to be transferred to the new owner. The new owner needs to register the car in the state where it will be driven. You may want to limit the use of the car until it is transferred to the beneficiary. If the decedent's car is involved in an accident before the car is transferred to the new owner, then the decedent's Estate may be liable for the damage. Having adequate insurance on the car may save the Estate from monetary loss, but a pending lawsuit could delay Probate and prevent any money from being distributed to the beneficiaries until the lawsuit is settled.

If there is a Probate proceeding then it is the Personal Representative's job to transfer the motor vehicles to the proper beneficiary. If the decedent was survived by a spouse, then under Minnesota law, the surviving spouse is entitled to at least one of the decedent's automobiles (MN 524.2-403) (see page 94).

If the decedent was single and made a specific gift of his car in his Will, the Personal Representative will transfer the car to that person. If there was no mention of the car in the decedent's Will, then the car goes to the *residuary beneficiaries* under the Will, i.e., those who inherit whatever is left once all the bills have been paid and all the special gifts made in the Will are distributed.

If the decedent did not have a Will, then the car goes to the decedent's heirs as determined by Minnesota's Laws of Intestate Succession.

TRANSFER WHEN MORE THAN ONE BENEFICIARY

If there is more than one person who has the right to inherit the car, then they all can take title to the car. That may not be a practical thing to do since only one person can drive the car at any given time and if one gets into an accident, they all can be held liable. The better route is for the beneficiaries to agree to have one person take title to the car. The person taking title will need to compensate the others for their share of the car. In such case the beneficiaries need to come to an agreement as to the value of the car.

DETERMINING THE VALUE OF THE CAR

Cars are valued in different ways. The **collateral** value of the car is the value that banks use to evaluate the car for purposes of making a loan to the owner of the car. If you were to trade in a car for the purpose of purchasing a new car, the car dealer would offer you the **wholesale** value of the car. Were you to purchase that same car from a car dealer, then he would price it at its **retail** or **fair market value**. Usually the retail price is highest, wholesale is lowest and the collateral value of the car is somewhere in between.

You can call your local bank to get the collateral value of the car. It may be more difficult to obtain the wholesale value of the car because the amount of money a dealer is willing to pay for the car depends on the value of the new car that you are purchasing. You can determine the car's retail value by looking at comparable used car advertisements in the local newspaper. Rather than going through the effort of determining these three values, you can use your Internet search engine to look up the Kelly Blue Book. This publication gives Low, Average and High Blue Book Values which corresponds to the wholesale, collateral and retail values.

⬤ MAKING THE TRANSFER ⬤

To transfer the car you will need to go to the Motor Vehicle Registrar office in the county of the decedent's residence. You can find the address and telephone number of each county office on the Internet:

 MINNESOTA DEPARTMENT OF SAFETY
http://www.dps.state.mn.us

If you are the surviving spouse, then all you need do is bring in a certified copy of the death certificate, the original Certificate of Title, and your own driver's license to identify yourself, and the Clerk will have the Certificate of Title transferred to your name. If you are the Personal Representative, you need to bring in the original Certificate of Title, your Letters and your own identification. If you are the beneficiary of the car and no Probate proceeding is necessary, the Clerk will require that you sign a Surviving Heir Affidavit. You may want to call the Driver and Vehicle Services at (651) 296-6911 for information about what documents you need to bring with you. You may want to call the Department of Safety to determine the cost of making the transfer. Their toll free number is (888) 871-3171.

CANCELING THE DRIVER'S LICENSE

It is important to notify the Department of Public Safety of the death and to turn in the decedent's driver's license or photo ID. You can do this by writing "Deceased" across the driver's licence and mailing it and a certified copy of the death certificate to the nearest Motor Vehicle Registrar's Office or to **DRIVER AND VEHICLE SERVICES**
445 Minnesota Street
St. Paul, Minnesota   55101
The Department will take the decedent off their mailing list. This will assist the Department in preventing others from using the decedent's name for fraudulent purposes.

TRANSFERRING THE MOBILE HOME

A mobile home is transferred the same as any other motor vehicle. Before transferring the motor vehicle, you need to find out whether the land on which the mobile home is located was leased or owned by the decedent. If the decedent was renting space in a trailer park, then you need to contact the trailer park owner to transfer the lease agreement to the beneficiary of the mobile home. If the decedent owned the land under the mobile home, then a Probate proceeding will be necessary to transfer the land to the proper beneficiary. See page 140 for information about transferring real property.

TRANSFERRING THE SNOWMOBILE AND/OR WATERCRAFT

All snowmobiles and watercraft must be registered with the Commissioner of Natural Resources. To transfer the snowmobile or watercraft to the proper beneficiary, the Personal Representative must issue a bill of sale to the beneficiary on a form authorized by the Commissioner. The new owner must then obtain his own registration for the snowmobile or watercraft. He can do so by taking the bill of sale to the nearest Deputy Registrar of Motor Vehicles (MN 84.82).

If no Probate proceeding is necessary, and the decedent's Probate Estate is less than $20,000, the beneficiary of the snowmobile or watercraft can obtain title to the vehicle by using the Small Estate Affidavit as described later in this chapter. You can get information from the Department of Natural Resources Information Center by calling (888) 646-6367 or visiting their Web site.

 DEPARTMENT OF NATURAL RESOURCES
http://www.dnr.state.mn.us

The leased car is not an asset of the Estate because the decedent did not own the car. The leased car is a liability to the Estate because the decedent was obligated to pay the balance of the monies owed on the lease agreement. The Personal Representative, or next of kin, need to work out an agreement with the company to either assign the lease to a beneficiary who agrees to pay for the lease, or to have the Estate pay off the lease by purchasing the car under the terms of the lease agreement.

Some lenders will allow the lease to be assigned to a beneficiary provided the Estate remains liable for the balance of payment. In such case, it is better to have the beneficiary refinance the car and have the original lease agreement paid in full.

If the remaining payments exceed the current market value of the car, there may be a temptation to hand the keys over to the leasing company. This may not be the best strategy, because the leasing company can sell the car and then sue the Estate for the balance of the monies owed. If the decedent had no assets or if the only assets he had are creditor proof, then simply returning the car may be an option. But if the decedent's Estate has assets available to pay the balance of the lease payments, then the Personal Representative needs to arrange to have the car transferred in a way that releases the Estate from all further liability.

INCOME TAX REFUNDS

Any refund due to the decedent under a joint federal income tax return filed by his surviving spouse will be sent to the surviving spouse. If the decedent's Personal Representative filed the final return, then the refund check will be sent to him to be deposited to the Estate account.

If the decedent was single and no Probate proceeding is necessary, then whoever is entitled to the decedent's Estate is entitled to the refund check. If you are the beneficiary of the decedent's Estate, you can obtain the refund by filing IRS form 1310 along with the decedent's final income tax return (the 1040). You can obtain form 1310 from the decedent's accountant, or if he did not have an accountant and you wish to file yourself, you can call the IRS at (800) 829-3676 to obtain the form. You can get instructions, publications and forms from the Internal Revenue Service Web site:

IRS WEB SITE
IRS FORMS AND INSTRUCTIONS
http://www.irs.ustreas.gov/prod/forms_pubs/forms.html
IRS PUBLICATIONS
http://www.irs.ustreas.gov/prod/forms_pubs/pubs.html

The Personal Representative does not need to file form 1310 because once he files the decedent's final income tax return, any refund will be forwarded to him. Similarly, it is not necessary for the surviving spouse who filed a joint return to file form 1310.

The decedent's final Minnesota income tax return needs to be filed at the same time the federal income tax return is filed (MN 289A.18). The surviving spouse can file a joint return, and will receive the check if any refund is due. If there is no surviving spouse, then the Personal Representative has the responsibility of filing the final tax return. If no Probate proceeding is necessary, then the next of kin can file the return. If you have any question about filing the decedent's final return, you can call (800) 652-9094. TTY users call (651) 297-2196.

You can also find information about filing on behalf of a deceased taxpayer at the Minnesota Department of Revenue Web site:

 MINNESOTA DEPARTMENT OF REVENUE WEB SITE
http://www.taxes.state.mn.us

DEPOSITING THE TAX REFUND

A refund check sent to the Personal Representative will be deposited into the Estate account. If no Probate proceeding has been started and the refund check (or any other check) is in the name of the decedent, you can deposit it into the decedent's bank account. You can get the money in the decedent's account by using whatever Probate proceeding is appropriate. If the amount in the account is not more than $20,000, then you use the procedure described on the next page.

TRANSFERS OF $20,000 OR LESS

No Probate proceeding is necessary if the value of all personal property held in the decedent's name only is $20,000 or less. Whoever is entitled to the property can get possession of the item by means of an Affidavit prepared according to Minnesota Statute 524.3-1201. A sample Affidavit appears on the next page. It is appropriate to use the Affidavit to transfer monies owed to the decedent, his bank accounts, securities and the contents of a safe deposit box. And it can be used whether or not the decedent left a Will or not.

▶ YOU NEED PERMISSION FROM OTHER BENEFICIARIES ◀

The *Successor* of the decedent's Estate can use the Affidavit to get possession of the property. If the decedent left a Will then the beneficiaries of the Will are the Successors. If he died without a Will, his next of kin as defined by the Minnesota's Laws of Intestate Succession are the Successors (MN 524.1-201). If there are two Successors, they can sign a joint Affidavit to get the property. If several people are entitled to receive some part of the Estate, you will need their written permission to take possession of the property If one of the Successors refuses to give you permission, or if you are unable to contact a Successor or if you are not 100% sure of the identity of each and every Successor, you cannot use the Affidavit, and a Probate proceeding will be necessary.

▶ THE TRANSFER CAN BE REFUSED ◀

The person in possession of the decedent's property needs to be reasonably certain of your identity and your right to the possession of the property. The person or financial institution in possession of the property might refuse to make the transfer if they get Affidavits from more than one person, or if they are concerned that there is fraud or misrepresentation. In such case, a Probate proceeding will be necessary in order to get possession of the property.

AFFIDAVIT PURSUANT TO MINNESOTA STATUTE 524.3-1202

State of Minnesota

County of _____

_____ , the Affiant, first being duly sworn on oath, deposes and say that:

1. Affiant resides at

_____

in the State of _____ that his business is that of

_____

2. The decedent _____ died on _____
   A certified copy of the death certificate is attached as Exhibit A.

3. Thirty (30) days have elapsed since the death of the decedent or, in the event the property to be delivered is the contents of a safe deposit box, 30 days have elapsed since the filing of the inventory of the contents of the box pursuant to Minnesota Statute 55.10, paragraph (h).

4. The value of the entire probate estate, wherever located, including specifically any contents of a safe deposit box, less liens and encumbrances, does not exceed $20,000

5. To the best of Affiant's knowledge and belief no application or petition for appointment of Personal Representative is pending or has been granted in any jurisdiction.

6. Affiant is the claiming successor and is entitled to payment or delivery of the property described as follows:

_____

_____
Affiant

Subscribed and sworn to before me on this ____day of_____

_____
Notary Public

IS THIS TOO GOOD TO BE TRUE?

This seems almost too easy. The reader may be thinking "You mean that all I need to do is go to a brokerage office, or bank, give them an Affidavit and they will hand over the decedent's personal property?"

The answer is "yes, but..."

▶ LIABILITY FOR DECEDENT'S DEBTS ◀

Before using the Affidavit, you need to either pay all of the decedent's debts or see to it that arrangements have been made for their payment. But it could happen that the decedent owed money that you know nothing about. Any creditor can come forward and demand payment from whomever has possession of the decedent's property (that's you) (MN 524.3-901).

If you suspect that there may not be sufficient funds in the Probate Estate to pay all debts, it is better to have a full Probate proceeding and let the Court decide how much each creditor is paid. Once appointed, the Personal Representative can require that anyone who inherited funds as joint owner or as a named beneficiary of the account to contribute their share of monies owed (see page 84). If you just take possession of the property without going through Probate you will not have any authority to require contributions to pay the debt from the beneficiary of the account.

Better to let the Personal Representative settle the Estate if there is any chance that there may be a creditor problem. The Personal Representative can follow the directions of the Court without any personal liability to himself or to the beneficiaries of the Estate. All of the beneficiaries can walk away from the situation without fear of being personally hounded to pay for the decedent's debts.

TRANSFERRING REAL PROPERTY

No Probate proceeding is necessary to transfer real property if the decedent held that property:

⇨ as the owner of a Life Estate - or -

⇨ jointly with rights of survivorship

Nothing need be done to establish that the surviving party now owns the property, however, the decedent's name remains on the deed. Anyone examining title to the property will not know of the death. It is the job of the Minnesota Department of Health to issue the death certificate, but not to publish it or make it part of the public record. Of course, if there is a Probate proceeding, anyone can look up those public records and learn of the death. But with or without a Probate procedure it is a good idea to have your attorney prepare an ***Affidavit Of Identification and Survivorship*** for you to sign. Your attorney will attach a certified copy of the death certificate to the Affidavit and then forward the documents to the Office of the County Recorder in the county where the property is located. If your property is registered under the Torrens System your attorney can arrange for a new Certificate of Title to be issued that identifies you as the current owner.

If the decedent held real property in his name only or jointly with another as Tenants in Common, then a Probate proceeding is necessary. The attorney for the Personal Representative will prepare and record a ***Deed of Distribution*** transferring the property to the proper beneficiary. If you are the beneficiary of that property, you should receive the original recorded Deed of Distribution for your records.

TRANSFERRING OUT OF STATE PROPERTY

Each state regulates the transfer of real property within that state. Some states such as Ohio have rules much like Minnesota. They record an Affidavit to show that a joint owner, or owner of a Life Estate is now deceased.

In other states, such as Washington, it is the practice not to record any document, but just keep a certified copy of the death certificate available to present at closing when the property is transferred.

A few states, such as Florida, allow the death certificate to be recorded in the county where the property is located, so that anyone who examines title to the property will know that the Grantee is deceased. In Florida, the Clerk of the Circuit Court is in charge of recording deeds and death certificates. In other states, it may be the County Registrar or the County Recorder. You may want to call the recording department in the county where the property is located to find out what documents (if any) need to recorded to let people know that the surviving joint tenant, or the remainder Grantee of a Life Estate deed, now owns the property.

Of course if the decedent owned real property in his own name or as a Tenant In Common, you need to contact an attorney in that state to have the property transferred to the proper beneficiary.

There needs to be a Probate proceeding if the decedent left real property in his name only or as a Tenant-In-Common; or personal property worth more than $20,000. Probate can take anywhere from several months to more than a year depending on the size and complexity of the Probate Estate.

There are different ways to conduct the Probate proceedings. A **Formal Probate** is conducted when there is some issue raised that requires the Court to decide the matter, such as a Will contest, or a dispute as to who is to be appointed as Personal Representative. If there is no dispute that needs to be resolved by the Court, then an **Informal Probate** proceeding can be conducted.

THE SUMMARY PROCEEDING

A **Summary Proceeding** is a shortened Probate proceeding that is conducted when the value of the Probate Estate is $100,000 or less, not counting the value of the homestead and personal property that are exempt from the claims of creditors (see Pages 94, 95). The judge will decide if it is necessary to appoint a Personal Representative. If there are enough funds to pay monies owed by the decedent, the allowance for the spouse and children, funeral and administration expenses, the Court can just order that these items be paid and whatever remains distributed to the proper beneficiary (MN 524.3-1203).

SUPERVISED VS. UNSUPERVISED ADMINISTRATION

Some Wills require that the Probate proceeding be supervised by the Court; but most often, the Personal Representative does the job of settling the Estate independently and without seeking permission from the Court.

Supervised or unsupervised, Minnesota statute 524.3-715 identifies some 29 things the Personal Representative can do without seeking Court permission, including:

⇨   paying for the funeral, cost of last illness, debts and taxes and all of the costs of administration;

⇨   employing persons, including attorneys, auditors, investment advisors, even if they are associated or related to the Personal Representative;

⇨   abandoning property, when in his opinion, the property is valueless or of no benefit to the Estate;

⇨   borrowing money to be repaid from the Estate assets;

⇨   advancing money for the protection of the Estate;

⇨   insuring the assets against damage, loss or liability;

⇨   making a fair and reasonable compromise with anyone who owed money to the decedent;

⇨   making any type of repair to Estate property;

⇨   entering into a lease, even if the term of the lease extends beyond the Probate proceeding.

If the Court has ordered a Supervised Proceeding, the Personal Representative must seek Court permission to close the Estate and make the final distribution to the beneficiaries of the Estate. No Court approval is required to close the Estate and distribute property in an Unsupervised Proceeding (MN 524.3-501, 524.3-504, 524.3-1003).

YOUR RIGHTS AS A BENEFICIARY

If you are a beneficiary of the decedent's Estate, then it is important that you know what rights you have and, when necessary, how to assert those rights.

✧ RIGHT TO BE INFORMED

You are entitled to receive a copy of any document that is filed during the Probate of the Estate. Before or during the Probate proceedings, you can file a **DEMAND FOR NOTICE** with the Court. Once this document is filed, you will be notified of any proceeding that comes before the Court.

✧ RIGHT TO YOUR OWN ATTORNEY

The attorney who handles the Estate is employed by, and represents, the Personal Representative. If the Estate is sizeable, then you might consider employing your own attorney to check that things are done properly and in a timely manner. Even with a small Estate, you may want to consult with an attorney if at any time you are concerned about the way the Probate is being conducted.

✧ RIGHT TO COPY OF WILL

You can obtain a copy of the Will as soon as it is filed with the Court. If you have any concern about the validity of the Will you can raise an objection; and the Court will conduct a Formal proceeding to resolve the matter (MN 524.3-401, 524.3-402).

A Formal Probate proceeding can be stressful and time consuming. Before raising an objection to this or any other part of the Probate proceeding, it is important to consult with an attorney who is experienced in Probate matters.

The attorney can explain the best way for you to present your concerns to the Court. He can tell you what arguments will sway the Court, and what arguments have such little probability of succeeding that they are not worth pursuing.

✧ RIGHT TO DEMAND SUFFICIENT BOND

It doesn't happen often, but every now and again a Personal Representative will run off with Estate funds. A bond is insurance for the Estate. If Estate monies are stolen then the company that issued the bond will reimburse the Estate for the loss.

Most Wills direct that no bond be required. The reason for a not requiring a bond is two-fold. The Will maker chooses someone he trusts to administer the Estate, so he does not think a bond is necessary. And there are economic reasons. The cost of the bond is paid with Estate funds, and ultimately the amount inherited is reduced by the amount paid for the bond.

Even though the Will directs that no bond be given, the Court may order a bond if the Representative is a resident of another state, or if the Court finds that the Personal Representative is disreputable or unreliable. You, as a beneficiary, have the right to ask the Court to require a bond if you have concerns about the safety of the property. To make the request you need to file a written demand that the Personal Representative give bond. You will need to mail a copy of the demand to the Personal Representative (MN 524.3-603, 524.3-605).

The Court will investigate the matter and decide whether or not to grant your request. You have the right to go before the Court and explain your position, but before doing so, you should consult with a Probate attorney.

✧ RIGHT TO REQUEST A SUPERVISED ADMINISTRATION

As explained, the Personal Representative can go about the business of settling the decedent's Estate without asking Court permission to do so. If the administration is Unsupervised, he can even close the Estate without having the Court check to see that things were done properly. You, as a beneficiary of the Estate, have the right to request a Supervised Probate proceeding. If the decedent's Will directs that the Probate proceedings be Unsupervised, the Court will not order a Supervised proceeding unless the Court finds it is necessary to protect those affected by the Probate proceedings. Again it is important to consult with an experienced Probate attorney before deciding to request a Supervised Probate proceeding (MN 524.3-502).

✧ RIGHT TO CHALLENGE THE ATTORNEY'S FEES

The Personal Representative has the right to employ an attorney to guide him through the procedure so that things will be done properly and at no personal cost to the Representative. It is proper to have the attorney paid with Estate funds. There is no statutory guideline for what is a "reasonable" fee for the Personal Representative's attorney. You can ask the Personal Representative what attorney fees you can expect to be charged to the Estate.

If you think the fees charged by the attorney are excessive, you can ask the Court to review compensation paid to the attorney or to anyone else employed by the Personal Representative during the Probate proceeding. This includes monies paid to accountants, investment advisors, appraisers, etc. If the Court finds that the person was over-paid, the Court can order that monies be refunded (MN 524.3-715, 524.3-721).

But it isn't all that simple to challenge monies paid to professionals as part of the administration of the Estate. The Court will not disturb the contractual arrangement between the professional (attorney, accountant, etc.) and his client (the Personal Representative) unless the Court finds that the fee paid are unreasonable. It is important to consult with your own attorney if you decide to challenge fees paid by the Personal Representative to administer the Estate.

✧ RIGHT TO CHALLENGE PERSONAL REPRESENTATIVE'S FEE

The Personal Representative has a right to reasonable compensation for his efforts in settling the Estate (MN 524.3-719). If the Personal Representative is also a beneficiary of the Estate, he may decide not to take a fee and just take his inheritance. The reason may be economic. Any fee the Representative takes is taxable as ordinary income, but monies inherited are not taxable to him as a beneficiary.

Ask the Personal Representative to tell you, in writing, whether he intends to ask for a fee, and if so, how much. There are no statutory guidelines for what is a "reasonable" fee for the Personal Representative. If you think the amount charged is unreasonable, you can follow the same proceeding as suggested for attorney fees; i.e., ask the Court to set a hearing on the matter. You can expect the Personal Representative, and his attorney, to contest your objection to the amount being charged, so you'd be wise to have your own attorney represent you at the hearing.

✧ RIGHT TO COPY OF INVENTORY

The Personal Representative must prepare an inventory of the assets of the Probate Estate within 6 months of his appointment or within 9 months of the date of death, whichever is the later. He is required to file the inventory with the Clerk of the Probate Court and to mail a copy to the surviving spouse and/or the residuary beneficiaries of the Estate. If you are the beneficiary of a specific gift and not one of the residuary beneficiaries, you can ask the Personal Representative (or his attorney) to mail you a copy as well (MN 524.3-706).

The Personal Representative is not required to employ an appraiser, but if he does, then the name and address of the appraiser must be indicated on the inventory. If you disagree with the value assigned to any item, you can ask to have an appraisal of the item to determine its fair market value as of the date of death (MN 524.3-707).

✧ RIGHT TO RECEIVE A DEBT FREE INHERITANCE

Once you receive your inheritance, about the last thing you want to hear is that there is some unfinished business, or worse yet that monies need to be paid from monies you just received. But that is just what could happen if the Personal Representative makes a distribution before all the taxes and creditors are paid (MN 524.3-909). You can protect yourself from this unhappy situation by checking to see that all of the decedent's creditors were paid and that all tax returns were filed and taxes paid.

✧ RIGHT TO AN ACCOUNTING

The Personal Representative can close the Estate any time after the time for filing claims is over (4 months from publication of Notice to Creditors). Before closing the Estate, the Personal Representative needs to file an accounting of how Estate funds were spent, and how the Personal Representative intends to distribute whatever funds are left (MN 524.3-1002, 524.3-1003).

You may be asked to sign a waiver of your right to an accounting, but keep in mind that the accounting is for your benefit. There are few situations that justify giving up your right to know how Estate monies were spent.

You should receive a copy of the accounting and proposed distribution. If the Estate has significant assets, you may want your own accountant to review the accounting. The Personal Representative will propose a distribution as directed in the Will or if no Will according to the Laws of Intestate Succession. Under Minnesota law, the beneficiaries of the decedent's Estate have the right to change the way the property is distributed by deciding, among themselves, how they wish to divide the Estate. To do so they need to sign a contract and give it to the Personal Representative. He will distribute the Estate according to that contract, provided, the agreement does not interfere with the rights of any creditor or any other beneficiary who did not sign the contract (MN 524.3-912).

✧ RIGHT TO RECEIVE INHERITANCE IN A TIMELY MANNER

As discussed, the Personal Representative can close the Estate any time after 4 months from the date of publication of the Notice to Creditors. If there are sufficient monies in the Estate to pay all debts, the beneficiaries of the Estate can ask the Personal Representative to distribute the Estate assets to the proper beneficiary at that time. If an Estate Tax return has been filed, it may take several months before the Personal Representative knows how much taxes need to be paid. In such case, you might ask the Personal Representative to make a partial distribution, i.e., to give the beneficiaries some of their inheritance now and the rest after the taxes have been paid.

If a year has passed, and you know that all bills and taxes have been paid, you can ask the Personal Representative the reason for the delay in settling the Estate. If he does not have a reasonable explanation ("I'm busy" is not reasonable), you can ask the Court to order that the property be distributed (MN 524.3-1002). You can do so by filing a petition asking the Court to order that the Personal Representative do a final accounting and close out the Estate. Once the petition is filed, he Court will conduct a hearing on the matter. The Personal Representative may argue against you at the hearing, and the Court may decide to give the Personal Representative more time to settle the Estate.

Court hearings can increase the cost of the Probate. It is important to consult with your attorney before deciding to file the petition. It may save money in the long run if your attorney can negotiate with the Personal Representative's attorney and come to an agreement about when the assets will be distributed.

IT'S YOUR RIGHT - DON'T BE INTIMIDATED

As a beneficiary, you have many legal rights, but you may feel uncomfortable asserting those rights with a friend or family member who is Personal Representative. Don't be. It's your money and your legal right to be kept informed. Be especially firm if the Personal Representative waves you off with:

"You've known me for years. Surely you trust me."

People who are trustworthy don't ask to be trusted. They do what is right. The very fact that the Personal Representative is resisting is a red flag. In such situation, you can explain that it is not a matter of trust, but a matter of what is your legal right. At the same time, keep things in perspective. Your relationship with the Personal Representative may be more important to you than the money you inherit. The job of settling an Estate can be complex and demanding. If the Personal Representative is getting the job done, then let him know that you appreciate his efforts.

THE CHECK LIST

We have discussed many things that need to be done when someone dies in the state of Minnesota. The next two pages contain a check list that you may find helpful.

You can check those items that you need to do, and then cross them off the list once they are done. We made the list as comprehensive as possible, so many items may not apply in your case. In such case, you can cross them off the list or mark them *N/A* (not applicable).

Things to do

FUNERAL ARRANGEMENTS TO BE MADE
☐ AUTOPSY   ☐ ANATOMICAL GIFT
☐ DISPOSITION OF BODY OR ASHES

DEATH CERTIFICATE
☐ HAVE CERTIFICATE RECORDED
GIVE COPY TO: _____

_____

NOTICE OF DEATH
PEOPLE TO BE NOTIFIED _____

COMPANIES TO NOTIFY
☐ TELEPHONE COMPANY
    ☐ LOCAL CARRIER   ☐ LONG DISTANCE   ☐ CELLULAR
☐ NEWSPAPER (OBITUARY PRINTED)
☐ NEWSPAPER CANCELLED   ☐ deposit refund
☐ SOCIAL SECURITY
☐ INTERNET SERVER
☐ TELEVISION CABLE COMPANY
☐ POWER & LIGHT   ☐ deposit refund
☐ POST OFFICE
☐ OTHER UTILITIES (GAS, WATER)   ☐ deposit refund
☐ PENSION PLAN
☐ ANNUITY
☐ HEALTH INSURANCE COMPANY
☐ LIFE INSURANCE COMPANY
☐ HOME INSURANCE COMPANY
☐ MOTOR VEHICLE INSURANCE COMPANY
☐ CONDOMINIUM OR HOMEOWNER ASSOCIATION
☐ CANCEL SERVICE CONTRACT   ☐ **deposit refund**
☐ CREDIT CARD COMPANIES _____

_____

_____

Things to do

REMOVE DECEDENT AS BENEFICIARY OF:

☐ WILL   ☐ INSURANCE POLICY   ☐ PENSION PLAN
☐ BANK OR IRA ACCOUNT   ☐ SECURITY

DEBTS

PAY DECEDENT'S DEBTS (AMOUNT & CREDITOR)

_____

COLLECT MONIES OWED TO DECEDENT (AMOUNT & DEBTOR)

_____

TAXES

☐ FILE FINAL FEDERAL INCOME TAX RETURN
☐ FILE FINAL STATE INCOME TAX RETURN
☐ RECEIVE INCOME TAX REFUND
☐ FILE ESTATE TAX RETURN

PROPERTY TO BE TRANSFERRED

☐ PERSONAL EFFECTS
☐ MOTOR VEHICLE
☐ BANK ACCOUNT
☐ CREDIT UNION ACCOUNT
☐ IRA ACCOUNT
☐ SECURITIES
☐ BROKERAGE ACCOUNT
☐ INSURANCE PROCEEDS
☐ HOMESTEAD
☐ TIME SHARE
☐ OTHER REAL PROPERTY
☐ CONTENTS OF SAFE DEPOSIT BOX

OTHER THINGS TO DO

_____
_____
_____

WHAT TO KEEP — WHAT TO THROW AWAY

Once the Probate proceeding is over, you will be left with many documents and wonder which you need to keep:

COURT DOCUMENTS

You should keep a copy of the inventory to establish the value of property that you inherit. That value becomes your basis for any Capital Gains tax that you may need to pay in the future. You may also want to keep a copy of the Decree of Distribution which is a statement of what money and property was given to each beneficiary. Other than these documents, there is no reason to keep any Court document, provided you are satisfied with the way things were done, and do not intend to take action against the Personal Representative or his attorney. The Clerk of the Probate Court keeps the Probate file on record, so if for some reason you need a copy of a Probate document, you can get it from the Clerk.

PERSONAL DOCUMENTS

You may wish to keep the decedent's personal papers (birth certificate, marriage certificate, naturalization papers, army records, religious documents, etc.) for your own personal records. You may want to keep the decedent's medical records in the event that a member of the family needs to check out a genetic disease.

TAX RECORDS

The IRS has up to three years to collect additional taxes, and you have up to 7 years to claim a loss from a worthless security, so you should keep the decedent's tax file for seven years from the date of filing the return. You can learn more about which records to keep from the IRS publication 552. You can get the publication by calling the IRS at (800) 829-3676 or you can download it from their Web site: http://www.irs.gov.

Everyman's Estate Plan 7

The first six chapters of this book describe how to wind up the affairs of the decedent. As you read those chapters, you learned about the kinds of problems that can occur when settling the decedent's Estate. It is relatively simple for you to set up an Estate Plan so that your family members are not burdened with similar problems. An *Estate Plan* is the arranging of your finances for maximum control and protection during your lifetime, and at the same time ensuring that your property will be transferred quickly and at little cost to your heirs.

If you think that only wealthy people need to prepare an Estate Plan, you are mistaken. Each year, heirs of relatively modest Estates, spend thousands of dollars to settle an Estate. A bit of planning could have eliminated most, if not all, of the expense and hassle suffered by those families.

The suggestions in this chapter are designed to assist the average person in preparing a practical and inexpensive Estate Plan, so we named this chapter EVERYMAN'S ESTATE PLAN.

Once you create your own Estate Plan, you can be assured that your family will not be left with more problems than happy memories of you.

AVOIDING PROBATE

(   )   If you have a Will, then there will need
        to be a Probate administration.
(   )   Probate will be necessary if you don't have a Will.
(   )   Probate is necessary if you leave anything worth
        more than $20,000.

If you answered false to all of the above, you are either a lawyer, or you carefully read chapters 5 and 6.

For those who do not enjoy "Pop Quizzes," please forgive our reversion to teacher. The point we were attempting to make is that:

> Whether a Probate procedure is necessary has nothing to do with whether there is a Will, or even how much money is involved. The determining factor is how the property is titled (owned).

There are three ways to title property:
- ✧   jointly with another
- ✧   in trust for another
- ✧   in your name only.

In general, property held jointly or in trust for someone goes directly to the intended beneficiary without the need for Probate. There may need to be a Probate proceeding if property is held in the decedent's name only.

In this chapter we explore the pros and cons of titling property in each of the three ways, beginning with holding property jointly with another.

OWNERSHIP OF BANK ACCOUNTS

You can arrange to have all of your bank accounts set up so that should you die, the money goes directly to a beneficiary. For example, suppose all you own is a bank account and you want whatever you have in the account to go to your son and daughter when you die. You might think that a simple solution is to put each child's name on the account as joint tenants, but first consider the problems associated with a joint account.

☒ POTENTIAL LIABILITY

If you hold a bank account jointly with your adult child and that child is sued or gets a divorce, the child may need to disclose his ownership of the joint account. In such a case, you may find yourself spending money to prove that the account was established for your convenience only and that all of the money in that account really belongs to you.

☒ OVERREACHING

If you set up a joint account with your child so that the child has authority to withdraw funds from the account, then funds could be withdrawn without your knowledge or authorization (MN 524.6-208).

If you open a multiple party account with two of your children, then there is the problem of what happens to the funds after your death. Should you die, then unless you make some other provision in your Will, your share of the account belongs to the surviving joint owners, equally (MN 524.6-204, 524.6-209). But as a practical matter each joint owner has free access to the joint account. After your death the first child to the bank may decide to withdraw all of the money and that will, at the very least, cause hard feelings between them.

Holding a bank account jointly with your beneficiary eliminates the need for Probate, but at the cost of control of the funds. You can title your bank account so that it passes directly to your beneficiary, but without allowing access to the account during your lifetime. When you open your account you can direct the bank to hold your account *In Trust For* ("ITF") a beneficiary that you name; or you can have a contract with the bank directing the bank to *Pay On Death* ("POD") all of the money in the account to one or more beneficiaries that you name.

The contract that you sign with the bank will give specific instructions that the bank will follow should you die while the account is open. If you open an In Trust For or Pay On Death account, then unless the contract with your bank states differently, under Minnesota law:

⇨   you are free to change beneficiaries without asking the beneficiary's permission to do so.

⇨   The beneficiary does not have any right to money in the account during your lifetime.

⇨   If you name two or more beneficiaries, the funds are divided equally between them upon your death. Unless your agreement with the bank states otherwise, if one of your beneficiaries dies before you do, the surviving beneficiary will inherit the account.

(MN 524.6-201, 524.6-203, 524.6-204).

The Minnesota law for securities is much the same as the statutes for bank accounts. You can arrange to have a security (a stock, bond or brokerage account) transferred to a beneficiary upon your death. You can instruct the holder of the security to PAY ON DEATH ("POD") or TRANSFER ON DEATH ("TOD") to a named beneficiary.

You can open a **TRANSFER ON DEATH** securities account with instructions to transfer your securities a beneficiary or his/her lineal descendants should the beneficiary die before you. For example:

Alice Lee TOD Wayne Lee LDPS

which is short-hand for:
"Alice Lee is the owner of the securities account. On her death, transfer all the securities in her account to Wayne Lee. If Wayne dies before Alice then give the securities to Wayne's lineal descendants, per stirpes."

The term "per stirpes" has the same meaning as the term "by representation" (see page 115).

The TOD account is much the same as the POD account. Wayne has no right to the securities until Alice dies. Alice is free to close the account or to change beneficiaries, without permission from Wayne (MN 524.6-305, 524.6-310).

There may be times when you wish to hold a security jointly (say with your spouse) and have your children inherit the security when you both die. For example:

ELDON CONNORS and LORRAINE CONNORS, JT TEN
TOD FRED CONNORS and MARIE CONNER

⇨   Fred and Marie have no right to the account during the lifetime of their parents.

⇨   Should Eldon or Lorraine die, then the surviving spouse owns the account, and is free to close the account or change the beneficiary of the account.

⇨   Should Fred die before his parents and the account is not changed, under Minnesota law, all of the money in the account will go to Marie. Should both Fred and Marie die before their parents, then the security will go to the Estate of the last parent to die (MN 524.6-304, 524.6-306, 524.6-310).

If your Estate consists only of bank accounts and/or securities, and you want all of your property to go to one or two beneficiaries without the need for Probate, but with maximum control and protection of your funds during your lifetime, then holding your property in any of these beneficiary forms:

"In Trust For"
"Pay-On-Death"
"Transfer-On-Death"

should accomplish your goal.

GIFT TO A MINOR CHILD

At the beginning of this chapter, we identified two problems with a joint account: potential liability if the joint owner is sued and overreaching by the joint owner. If you wish to make a gift to a minor child, then that presents still another problem. The POD and TOD account avoid the problem of potential liability and overreaching, but if the beneficiary of such account is a minor, there is the problem of the child having access to a large sum of money.

Under Minnesota law, if the amount in the account is under $10,000, the financial institution can transfer the funds to a trust company or to an adult member of the child's family, as Custodian of the gift until the child is an adult. If the amount exceeds $10,000, the financial institution will not transfer the funds without authorization from the Probate Court. The Court may decide to appoint a Conservator to care for the child's property (MN 527.26, 527.27).

You may think it best that the child inherits more than $10,000; this way a Court will see to it that the monies are held safely until the child is an adult. But that presents a new set of problems. It takes time, effort and money to set up a conservatorship. If you leave the child a significant amount of money, then the Conservator has the right to be paid to manage those funds. It could happen that the cost of the conservatorship significantly reduces the amount of money inherited by the child.

There are ways to avoid the problem of having a Conservator appointed to care for property inherited by a child, and yet ensuring that the monies are protected. One is the **Minnesota Uniform Transfers to Minors Act**. That law is described on the next page.

The Minnesota Uniform Transfers to Minors Act is designed to protect gifts made to a minor. You can appoint someone to be the Custodian of a gift given under the Uniform Transfers to Minors Act until that child reaches the age of 21. It is appropriate to use this method if you want to make a gift to the child in your Will, or if you want to make the child a beneficiary of your life insurance policy or pension plan (MN 527.23).

You can even use the Minnesota Uniform Transfers to Minors Law to make a gift during your lifetime of some item such as a shares in a corporation or a limited partnership interest. You can nominate yourself as Custodian of the gift, or you can name another person to serve as Custodian. Once the lifetime gift is made it becomes irrevocable, so this method is not appropriate unless you are sure that you want the child to have the gift once he/she reaches the age of 21 (MN 527.21, 527.24).

If you make a minor child beneficiary of a life insurance policy, you need to name a trusted relative or friend or even a financial institution to be the Custodian of the gift. If you wish to make a gift to a minor in your Will, you can appoint your Personal Representative as Custodian of the gift. For example:
"I give the sum of $20,000 to my Personal Representative
_____ (name) as custodian for
_____ (name of minor) under the
Minnesota Uniform Transfers to Minors Act" (MN 527.29).

The Personal Representative will give the gift to the child if the child is 21 or older. If the child is under 21, the Personal Representative will hold the gift, as Custodian, until the child reaches 21.

The Custodian needs to invest and manage the property in a responsible, prudent manner. He must keep records of all transactions made with custodial property; and make those records available for inspection by the child's parent, or legal representative, or the child, if the minor is 14 or older. If those records are not to their satisfaction, they can petition (ask) the Probate Court to require the Custodian to give an accounting (MN 527.32, 527.39).

The Custodian has the discretion to use the gift to care for the child. The Custodian can pay monies directly to the child, or can use the money for the child's benefit. The Custodian can refuse to use any of the monies for the child and just keep the funds invested until the child reaches 21. If the Custodian wants to keep the funds invested the child's parent, or his legal representative, or the child once he is 14, can ask the Judge of the Probate Court to order the Custodian to part with some or all of the money for the benefit of the child. The Judge will decide what is in the child's best interest and then rule on the matter (MN 527.34).

The Custodian is entitled to be paid for his effort each year (MN 527.35). If the gift is sizeable, the Custodian's fee can be sizeable. Before appointing a person or a financial institution as Custodian, it is best to come to a written agreement about what will be charged to manage the custodial property.

A gift made under the Minnesota Uniform Transfers to Minors Act is limited to one minor only (MN 527.30). If you want to give a single gift, such as a gift of real property to two or more children, then a Trust may be the better way to go.

We will discuss Trusts later in this chapter.

THE GIFT OF REAL PROPERTY

As explained in Chapter 5, if you own real property together with another, then who owns the property upon your death depends on how the Grantee is identified on the face of the deed. If you compare the Grantee clause of the deed to the examples on pages 105 through 107 you can determine who will inherit the property should you die. If you are not satisfied with the way the property will be inherited, then you need to consult with an attorney to change the deed so that it will conform to your wishes.

If you hold real property in your name only, once you die, a Probate proceeding will be necessary in order to transfer the property to the proper beneficiary. If your main objective is to avoid Probate, you can have an attorney change the deed so that it descends to your beneficiary without the need for Probate. As with bank and securities accounts there are different ways to do so, each with its own advantages and disadvantages.

JOINT OWNERSHIP
If you hold property in your name only, and wish to avoid Probate, you can have your deed changed so that you and a beneficiary are joint owners. If you do so, should either of you die, the other will own the property 100%. That avoids Probate, but by making that person joint owner, you are, in effect, making a gift of half of the property during your lifetime. You will not be able to sell that property without the beneficiary's permission. And if the beneficiary gives permission and the property is sold, the beneficiary will have the legal right to half of the proceeds of the sale. As explained on the next page, you may be creating tax problems as well.

You can arrange to sell your home without paying a Capital Gains tax (see page 36), but if you make someone joint owner of your home who does not live with you, a Capital Gains tax may need to be paid on the joint owner's share of the proceeds should you decide to sell the property.

CAUTION — GIFT OF HOMESTEAD

Some elderly parents worry that they may need nursing care at some time in the future and lose all of their life savings to pay for that care. The parent may decide that the best way to avoid Probate and protect the homestead from loss is to transfer the homestead to their child with the understanding that the parent will continue to live there until he/she dies. But this is just trading risks.

⊠ RISK OF LOSS

Property transferred to your child could be lost if the child runs into serious financial difficulties or gets sued. This is especially a risk if your child is a professional doctor, nurse, accountant, financial planner, attorney, etc.). If your child is (or gets) married, then this complicates matters even more so. If the child is divorced, the property may need to be included as part of the settlement agreement. This may be to your child's detriment because the child may need to share the value of the property with his/her ex-spouse. If you do not transfer the property, it cannot become part of the marital equation.

⊠ LOSS OF HOMESTEAD CREDITOR PROTECTION

Up to $200,000 of the value of your homestead is protected from your creditors during your lifetime. If your homestead is used primarily for agricultural purposes, then up to half a million is protected from your creditors. With the exception of mechanic's liens, property taxes and mortgages on your homestead, none of your creditors can force the sale of your property unless you owe them more than $200,000 (or $500,000 if you live on a farm). If you simply transfer your homestead to a child, you lose this creditor protection (MN 510.01, 510.02).

If you are married, then it is a double loss of creditor protection. Not only do you lose creditor protection for yourself, you lose it for your spouse as well. If you transfer your homestead to your child and he does not occupy that property as his homestead, then there is no homestead creditor protection whatsoever. The child's creditors can force the sale of the property (that's your home) for relatively small amounts of unpaid debts.

⊠ POSSIBLE LOSS OF GOVERNMENT BENEFITS

If you transfer property, then depending upon the value of the transfer, you could be disqualified from receiving Medicaid or Supplemental Security Income ("SSI") benefits for a substantial period of time. When a person applies for Medicaid, he must disclose if, within 3 years of his application, he transferred property for less than the full value (i.e. he gifted property). This reporting period extends to 5 years if the transfer was to a Trust. The Medicaid agency will compute a disqualification period depending on the value of the transfer. This can present a serious problem should you need extended nursing care during the disqualification period.

⊠ POSSIBLE GIFT TAX

If the value of the transfer is worth more than $11,000 you need to file a gift tax return. For most of us, this is not a problem because no gift tax need be paid unless the value of the property (plus the value of all gifts in excess of the Annual Gift Tax Exclusion that you gave over your lifetime) exceeds $1,000,000 (see Page 39). But if your Estate is in that tax bracket, you need to be aware that you are "using up" your exemption amount.

⊠ POSSIBLE CAPITAL GAINS TAX

There is no discussion in Congress to do away with the Capital Gains Tax. If you gift the property to the child, when he sells the property he will be subject to a Capital Gains Tax on the increase in value from the price you paid to the selling price at the time of the sale. If you do not make the gift during your lifetime, the child will inherit the property with a step-up in basis, i.e., he will inherit the property at its market value as of the date of death. Under today's tax structure and continuing until 2009, that step-up in basis is unlimited. If your child sells the property when it is inherited, no Capital Gains Tax is due regardless of how large the step-up in basis. In 2010, there will be a limit on amount that can be inherited free of the Capital Gains Tax but that limit is quite high so for most of us this is not a concern.

⊠ LOSS OF HOMESTEAD TAX CREDITS

Each home owner in Minnesota is entitled to a tax break for property that they occupy as their principal residence. In addition there are special property tax classifications for the elderly, blind and those with low incomes. If you put the deed in the beneficiary's name and that property is your homestead, then you will lose these tax breaks. It could cost more money in taxes to continue to live in your own home. If you decide to transfer your homestead to a beneficiary, before doing so, call the Minnesota Department of Revenue Assistance line (800) 654-9094 and ask them what will be the tax consequence of the proposed transfer.

Some of the problems mentioned can be solved by transferring your homestead to your beneficiary while keeping a Life Estate for yourself. In particular, you can keep your homestead tax classification and there will be a step-up in basis upon your death. But, there is still the downside of not being able to sell the property during your lifetime without the permission of those you named as Grantee on the deed; and if you sell the property each Grantee is entitled to some portion of the proceeds of the sale.

As you can see there is much to consider before changing title to real property. Before making any transfer of real property, it is important to consult with your accountant and/or attorney and/or certified financial planner, to examine all aspects related to the transfer. If you are considering transferring your homestead because of the your concern for the cost of future health care, then before doing so, consult with an Elder Law attorney. He can suggest ways to protect your assets, and still ensure that you receive the health care that you may require in your later years.

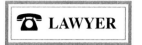 **LAWYER**   OUT OF STATE PROPERTY

Each state is in charge of the way property located in that state is transferred. If you own property in another state (or country) then you need to consult with an attorney in that state (or country) to determine how that property will be transferred to your beneficiaries once you die. Many state laws are similar to Minnesota, namely, property held as **JOINT TENANTS WITH RIGHT OF SURVIVOR** or with a **LIFE ESTATE INTEREST** are transferred without the need for Probate.

If you own property in another state in your name only, or as a **TENANT IN COMMON**, or if you hold property with your spouse in a community property state, then a Probate proceeding may need to be held in that state. If it is necessary to have a Probate proceeding in Minnesota, then a second Probate procedure may need to be held in the state where the property is located. This could have the effect of doubling the cost of Probate.

Still another problem is the matter of taxes. Inheritance taxes may be due in the state where the property is held. It may be necessary to file a tax return in two states. In addition to increased taxes, this can double the cost of the accounting fees.

You may wish to consult with an attorney for suggestions about how to set up your Estate Plan to avoid such problems.

A TRUST MAY BE THE SOLUTION (OR NOT)

A full Probate proceeding may be necessary if you hold property in your name only or as a Tenant-In-Common. We explored different ways to re-title property to avoid Probate, but these methods may have trade-offs that are unacceptable to you. One way to avoid many of these potential problems is to set up a ***Revocable Living Trust*** (also known as an ***Inter Vivos Trust***).

A Revocable Living Trust is designed to care for your property during your lifetime and then to distribute your property once you die without the need for Probate. You may have been encouraged to set up such a Trust by your financial planner, or attorney, or accountant. Even people of modest means are being encouraged to use a Trust as the basis of their Estate Plan. But Trusts have their pros and cons. Before getting into that, let's first discuss what a Trust is and how it works:

SETTING UP A TRUST

To create a Trust, an attorney prepares the Trust document in accordance with the client's needs and desires. The person who signs the document is called the ***Trustor*** or ***Settlor.*** If the ***Trustor*** also funds the Trust, then he is also referred to as the ***Grantor.*** We will refer to the Revocable Living Trust as the "Living Trust" or just the "Trust" and the person setting up the Trust as the "Grantor." The Trust document identifies who is to be the Trustee (manager) of property placed in the Trust. Usually the Grantor appoints himself as Trustee so that he is in total control of property that he places into the Trust. The Trust document also names a Successor Trustee who will take over the management of the Trust property should the Trustee resign, become disabled or die.

Once the Trust document is properly signed, the Grantor transfers property into the Trust. The Grantor does this by changing the name on the account from his individual name to his name as Trustee. For example, if Elaine Richards sets up a Trust naming herself as Trustee, and she wishes to place her bank account into the Trust then all she need do is instruct the bank to change the name on the account from ELAINE RICHARDS to:

ELAINE RICHARDS, TRUSTEE of the ELAINE RICHARDS REVOCABLE TRUST AGREEMENT DATED JULY 12, 2001.

When the change is made, all the money in the account becomes Trust property. Elaine (wearing her Trustee hat) has total control of the account, taking money out, and putting money in, as she sees fit. Similarly, if she wants to put real property into the Trust all she need do is have her attorney prepare a new deed with the Grantee identified as ELAINE RICHARDS, TRUSTEE (see page 107 for an example of real property placed into a Trust).

The Trust document states how the Trust property is to be managed during Elaine's lifetime. Should Elaine become disabled the Trust will provide for her Successor Trustee to take over and manage the Trust funds. Because the Trust is revocable, if she wishes, Elaine can terminate the Trust at any time and have all the Trust property returned and placed back into her own individual name. If she does not revoke her Trust during her lifetime, then once she dies the Trust becomes irrevocable, and her Successor Trustee must follow the terms of the Trust Agreement as written. If the Trust says to give the Trust property to certain beneficiaries, then the Successor Trustee will do so; and in most cases without any Probate proceeding. If the Trust directs the Successor Trustee to continue to hold property in Trust and use the money to take care of a member of Elaine's family, then the Successor Trustee will do so.

THE GOOD PART
Setting up a Trust has many good features.

☆ TAX SAVINGS:
Many people think that the Estate Tax will be phased out so that by 2010, no Estate Taxes will be due regardless of the size of an Estate. That's true for 2010, but the current law covers only the period from 2001 to 2010. The Estate Tax is scheduled to be reinstated on January 1, 2011 and Estates worth more than $1,000,000 will once again be subject to a sizeable Estate Tax. A couple with an Estate in excess of a million dollars can reduce the risk of an Estate Tax by setting up his and her Trusts, so that each person can take advantage of his own Exclusion value.

For example, if a couple own 2 million dollars, they can separate their funds into two Trusts each valued at one million dollars. Each Trust can be set up so that a surviving spouse can use the income from the deceased partner's Trust for living expenses. In this way, their standard of living need not be reduced by separating their funds into two Trusts. Once both partners are deceased, the beneficiaries of their respective Trusts will inherit the funds, hopefully with no Estate Tax due.

If the couple does not set up his/her Trusts and continue to hold their property jointly, then the last to die will own the two million dollars with only one tax Exclusion available.

☆ PRIVACY

Your Living Trust is a private document. No one but your Trustee and your beneficiaries need ever read it. If you leave property in a Will and there is a Probate proceeding, the Will must be filed with the court, where it becomes a public document. Anyone can go to the courthouse, read your Will and see who you did (or did not) provide for in your Will. Records in the Probate Court (inventories, creditor's claims, etc.) are open to public scrutiny. It is not much of a stretch to predict that in the future, Court records will be available on the Internet!

LEASE SAFE DEPOSIT BOX AS TRUSTEE

If you hold a safe deposit box in your name only, then once the bank learns of your death, they will restrict access to the box. The bank will allow your spouse or a beneficiary of your Estate to take an inventory of the contents of the safe deposit box, but only under the watchful eye of a company employee (see page 78). If the value of the contents of the safe deposit box exceed $20,000, a Personal Representative will need to be appointed just to get possession of the contents of your safe deposit box.

If you have arranged your finances to avoid Probate, it is self defeating to have entry to a safe deposit box trigger a Probate proceeding. One of the benefits of having a Living Trust, is that you can lease the safe deposit box in your name as Trustee. When you lease the safe deposit box you can have an agreement with the bank that they are to allow your Successor Trustee free access to the safe deposit box in the event of your incapacity or death.

☆ CARE FOR FAMILY MEMBER:

You can make provision in your Trust to care for a minor child or family member after you die. If your family member is immature or a born spender, you can include a Spendthrift provision to protect the beneficiary from squandering his inheritance. You can direct your Successor Trustee to use Trust funds to pay for the beneficiary's health care, education or living expenses, and nothing more.

You can set up a trust so that the creditors of the beneficiary cannot force the Trustee to use any of the Trust property to pay for monies owed by the beneficiary. Minnesota courts have even ruled that the Trust funds are protected from alimony and support payments; i.e., if the beneficiary of a spendthrift Trust owes alimony and/or back support, the Trustee has no duty to use Trust funds to make those payments. Of course, once the Trustee gives Trust funds to the beneficiary, his creditors can demand payment from the funds that are in the possession of the beneficiary (*Erickson v. Erickson*, 197 Minn. 71 (1936); 266 N.W. 161).

☆☆ AVOID PROBATE

In Minnesota, Probate can be time consuming and very expensive. Both the Personal Representative and his attorney are entitled to payment for their services. These fees can be significant. It may be necessary to employ accountants and appraisers, and financial planners as well. If you have property in two states, then two Probate proceedings may be necessary (one in each state) and that could have the effect of doubling the cost of Probate. If the Trust is properly drafted and your property transferred into the Trust, you should be able to avoid Probate altogether.

☆☆ AVOID APPOINTMENT OF A CONSERVATOR

Once you have a Trust you do not need to worry about who will take care of your property should you become disabled or too aged to handle your finances. The person you appoint as Successor Trustee will take over the care of the Trust property if you are unable to do so. If you do not have a Trust and you become incapacitated, a Court may need to appoint a Conservator to care for your property (MN 525.539). The cost to establish and maintain the conservatorship is charged to you. And that can be even more expensive than a full Probate proceeding.

The person appointed as your Conservator is entitled to be paid for his services. The amount paid must be approved by the Court. As a fiduciary, he/she is entitled to compensation just the same as any fiduciary such as a Personal Representative or a Trustee. The duties of a Conservator are much the same as those of a Personal Representative. He must take possession of your assets, file an inventory with the Court, and each year, account for monies spent. The Court may decide that a bond is necessary for the protection of your assets. If so, he will order the Conservator to obtain a bond.

As with a Personal Representative, the Conservator needs to employ an attorney to establish the conservatorship and see to it that it is properly administered. The Court may decide that you need legal representation; and if so, the Judge will appoint someone to protect your interests Attorney's fees must be approved by the Court. The hourly rate is much the same as the Court awards to attorneys to administer a Probate Estate (MN 525.551, 525.5501, 525.58).

Court filing fees, the cost of a bond, Conservator's fees, attorney's fees for you and the Conservator, are all paid from your Estate (that's your money!).

THE PROBLEMS

With all these perks, you may be ready to call your attorney to make an appointment to set up a Trust, but before doing so there are a few things you need to consider:

⊠   COMPLEXITY

A Trust is a fairly complex document, often more than 20 pages long. It needs to be that long because you are establishing a vehicle for taking care of your property during your lifetime, as well as after your death. The Trust usually is written in "legalese," so it may take you considerable time and effort to understand it. It is important to have your Trust document prepared by an attorney who has the patience to work with you until you fully understand each page of the document and are satisfied that what it says is what you really want.

⊠   TAXES MAY STILL BE A PROBLEM:

While the Grantor is operating the Trust as Trustee, all of the property held in a Revocable Living Trust is taxed as if the Grantor were holding that property in his/her own name. If the value of the Trust property exceeds the Estate Tax Exclusion and/or the Gift Tax Exclusion in effect at that time of the Grantor's death, taxes will be due and owing. For those in that fortunate tax bracket, an experienced Estate planner or tax attorney can suggest other, more advanced, Estate Planning strategies to reduce taxes.

⊠ PROBATE MIGHT STILL BE NECESSARY

The Trust only works for those items that you place in the Trust. If you have property that is held jointly with another, when you die, that property will go to the joint owner and not to the Trust. If you purchase a security in your name only, and forget to put it in your Trust, a Probate proceeding may be necessary to determine who should inherit that security.

The attorney who prepares the Trust will also create a safety net for such a situation. He prepares a Will for you sign at the same time you sign the Trust. The Will makes your Trust the beneficiary of your Probate Estate. If you own anything in your name only and a Probate proceeding should be necessary, the Will directs your Personal Representative to make that asset part of your Trust by transferring the asset to your Successor Trustee. Your Successor Trustee will add that asset to your Trust (MN 524.2-511).

The Will prepared by the attorney is called a "Pour Over Will" because it is designed to "pour" any asset titled in your name only, into the Trust. Having the Will ensures that all of your property will go to the beneficiaries named in your Trust. But the downside of holding property in your name only is that a Probate proceeding will be necessary to get that asset into your Trust. If avoiding Probate is your goal, holding property, in your name only, defeats that goal.

You can ensure that a Probate proceeding will not be necessary by transferring your assets into your Trust during your lifetime, but if you neglect to put something into your Trust, the Pour Over Will stands by to make the transfer of that asset into your Trust.

⊠ YOU MAY NEED YOUR SPOUSE'S PERMISSION
TO TRANSFER PROPERTY INTO YOUR TRUST

Most married couples prepare a Trust as part of their overall Estate Plan. Sometimes a married person has a Trust that was prepared prior to the marriage, or he may decide to create a Trust to care for children from a previous marriage. In such case, it may be necessary to have the spouse agree, in writing, to transfers into the Trust. The reason permission is needed is the *Elective Share*. The Grantor's spouse has a right to inherit at least as much as allowed under Minnesota law, unless the spouse has signed a waiver. The waiver can be included as part of prenuptial or postnuptial agreement, or it could be a separate document. To be effective, the waiver must be based on a full and fair disclosure of the finances involved, i.e., the spouse must be told knows what he/she is giving up by signing the waiver (MN 514.2-213).

There is a minimum Elective Share of $50,000. The surviving spouse can take that value or a percentage based on the length of the marriage. Minnesota statute 524.2-202 contains a table with the different percentages, starting at 3% for those married more than a year, but less than 3 years, to 50% for those married 15 years or more. The surviving spouse who has been married for one year or less is just entitled to the minimum value of $50,000.

The percentages given in the statute is not the percentage of the Probate Estate, but rather of the *Augmented Estate* as determined by Minnesota statute (MN 524.2-204, 524.2-205, 524.2-206).

The Augmented Estate includes the following:

⇨ The Probate Estate reduced by funeral and Probate expenses, homestead and family allowances and exemptions, and monies owed by the decedent;

⇨ Nonprobate transfers to the surviving spouse and others, such as joint bank accounts, Trust property, Transfer-On-Death securities, etc.; life insurance proceeds; pension funds;

⇨ Gifts in excess of $10,000 per person, per year, made by decedent (or his spouse) in the last two years of his life to someone other than the spouse.

⇨ Property owned by the surviving spouse

Notice that property belonging to the surviving spouse is included in the Augmented Estate. If the spouse's property is equal to or greater than that of the decedent, it could be that the surviving spouse is entitled to just the $50,000 minimum amount.

If your spouse is entitled to an Elective share and you make transfers into your Trust, or anywhere else, without your spouse's permission, your surviving spouse can go to the Probate Court and demand that as much property be transferred from your Trust (or from anyone in possession of your property) as is necessary to make up the Elective Share.

⊠ COST

Because of the thoroughness of the document and the fact that it is custom designed for you, a Trust will cost much more to draft than a simple Will. In addition to the initial cost of the Trust, it can be expensive to maintain the Trust should you become disabled or die. Your Successor Trustee has the right to charge for his duties as Trustee, as well as for any specialized service he performs. For example, if you choose an attorney to be Successor Trustee, the attorney has the right to charge to manage the Trust, and also to charge for any legal work he performs. A financial institution can charge to serve as Successor Trustee, and also charge to manage the Trust portfolio (MN 501B.71).

You could appoint a family member who may serve as Successor Trustee for little or no compensation. But regardless of whether you choose a professional or a family member to be Successor Trustee, you need to come to a written agreement as to what will be charged to manage the Trust. The fee agreement can be included in the Trust document with a provision that whoever accepts the job of Successor Trustee, agrees to accept the fee as provided in the Trust document.

⊠   NO CREDITOR PROTECTION

Because property held in a Revocable Living Trust is freely accessible to the Grantor, it is likewise accessible to his creditors. Although a Grantor can set up a Spendthrift Trust for the benefit of his family members, he cannot set up a Spendthrift Trust for himself. Trying to protect his funds through a Spendthrift Trust, would, in effect, be an attempt to defraud his creditors, and that is against Minnesota law (MN 570.02) .

⊠ ☆   THE TRUST IS LEGALLY ENFORCEABLE

Any beneficiary, or Trustee, of the Trust can petition the District Court to settle a dispute arising out of the administration of the Trust. If the Trustee is abusing his power or not accounting for Trust funds, the beneficiaries can ask the Court to have the Trustee removed (MN 501B.16).

We gave this section a cross and a star, because the right to have a Trust enforced or administered by a court is a double edged sword. It is great to have a court protect the rights of your beneficiaries, but the cost of a court battle could be greater than if your Estate was subject to Probate in the first place. Your beneficiaries are at a financial disadvantage because the Trustee can charge the legal expense of defending his actions to your Trust, but the beneficiaries must pay for the legal battle out of their own pocket.

The Court could require the Trustee to be personally liable for attorney's fees, but there would need to be some serious wrongdoing for that ruling.

MAYBE PROBATE ISN'T ALL THAT BAD

We explored many methods that can be used to transfer property without the need for Probate, it may be each method has a downside that is objectionable to you. Maybe you don't have enough money to warrant the cost of setting up the Trust at this time. Holding property jointly with another may raise issues of security and independence. Holding property so that it goes directly to a few beneficiaries in a Pay On Death account, may not be as flexible as you wish. This is especially the case if you wish to give gifts to several charities or to minor children instead of just one or two beneficiaries. For example, if you hold all your property so that it goes to your son without the need for Probate, and you ask him to use some of the money for your grandchild's education, it may be that your grandchild gets none of the money because your son is sued or falls on hard times. If you keep your property in your name only and leave a Will giving a certain amount of money for your grandchild, then the child will know exactly how much money you left and the purpose of that gift.

After taking into account all the pros and cons of avoiding Probate, you may well opt for a Will and a Probate proceeding. If you make such a decision, it is important to keep in mind that Estate Planning is not an "all or nothing" choice. You can arrange your Estate so that certain items pass automatically to your intended beneficiary, and other items can be left in your name only, to be distributed as part of a Probate proceeding. By arranging your finances in this manner, you can reduce the value of your Probate Estate, and that in turn should reduce the cost of Probate.

Your Minnesota Will

Many people decide that the Will is the best route to go but do not act upon it, thinking it unnecessary to prepare a Will until they are very old and about to die. But according to reports published by the National Center for Health Statistics (a division of the U.S. Department of Health and Human Services) 2 of every 10 people who die in any given year are under the age of 60.

Twenty percent may seem like a small number until it hits close to home as it did with a young couple. The couple was having difficulty conceiving a child. They went from doctor to doctor until they met someone just beginning his practice. With his knowledge of the latest advances in medicine, he was able to help them.

The birth of their child was a moment of joy and gratitude. They asked a nurse to take a picture of them all together — the proud parents, the newborn child and the doctor who made it all possible. Happiness radiated from the picture, but within 6 months, one of them would be dead.

You might think it was the child. An infant's life is so fragile. SIDS and all manner of childhood diseases can threaten a little one. But no, he grew up a healthy young man.

If you looked at the picture, you might guess the husband. Overweight and stressed out; his ruddy complexion suggested high blood pressure. He looked like a typical heart- attack-prone type A personality.

No, he was fine and went on to enjoy raising his son.

Probably the wife. She had such a difficult time with the pregnancy and the delivery was especially hard. Perhaps it was all too much for her. No, she recovered and later had two more children.

It was the doctor who was killed in a collision with a truck.

REASONS TO MAKE WILL

Though we all agree, that one never knows, still people put off making a Will figuring that if they die before getting around to it, Minnesota law will take over and their property will be distributed in the manner that they would have wanted anyway. The problem with that logic is the complexity of Minnesota's Laws of Intestate Succession. If you are survived by a spouse, child, parent or sibling, then it isn't too difficult to figure out who will inherit your property. But if none of these survive you, the ultimate beneficiary of your property may not be the person you would have chosen, had you taken the time to do so.

Others think that it is not necessary to have a Will because they have arranged their finances so that all of their property will be inherited without the need for Probate. But money could come into your Estate after your death. This could happen in any number of ways from winning the lottery and dying (of happiness, no doubt) to receiving insurance funds after your death. For example, if you die in a house fire or flood the insurance company may need to pay for damage done to your property. In such case, a Personal Representative may need to be appointed and the monies distributed according to Minnesota law.

If you die without a Will, the Personal Representative may not be the person you would have chosen. The monies may be distributed differently than you would have wished. And as explained on the next page, there are other important reasons to make a Will.

🗐 MAKE GIFTS OF YOUR PERSONAL PROPERTY

Another benefit to making a Will is that you can make provision for who will get your personal property, including your car. If you make a gift of your car in your Will, then it will be relatively simple for your car to be transferred to the beneficiary. If you do not make a specific gift of your car, then it becomes part of your Probate Estate. Your Personal Representative will decide what to do with the car. He can sell it and include the proceeds of the sale in the Estate funds to be distributed to your residuary beneficiaries; or he can give the car to one beneficiary of your Estate as part of that beneficiary's share of the Estate.

SMALL GIFTS MATTER

Many who have lost someone close to them report that the distribution of small personal items caused the greatest conflict. If you arrange your finances so that no Probate proceeding is necessary, your next of kin will need to decide how to distribute your personal effects. Without guidance from you and no Representative with authority to make decisions, there could be much disagreement and hard feelings, over items of little monetary value.

If you make a Will, then under Minnesota law, you can make gifts of your personal effects (record collection, books, jewelry etc.) by making a list of these gifts and attaching it to your Will. Your Personal Representative will distribute your personal effects according to that list. You can change the list at any time just so long as you sign and date the list. No witness to your signature is needed. The list is for items with more sentimental than monetary value. You should not include money gifts, securities or real property in the list. Those items need to be given as part of your Will (MN 524.2-513).

🗐 MAKE ADJUSTMENT FOR PRIOR GIFTS

With a Will you can make adjustments for gifts or loans given during your lifetime. For example, if you loaned money to a family member and do not expect to be repaid, you can deduct the loan from that person's inheritance. Of course, it may be that you are not concerned with inequities. That was the case of an aged woman with three children, Paul, Erika and Frank, her youngest. Frank always seemed to need some assist from his mother. She often "lent" him money that he never repaid. Her other children were responsible and independent. Paul was married and had children of his own. He decided to purchase a house but was having trouble accumulating the down payment. His mother agreed to lend him the money. Paul offered to give his mother a mortgage on the property. His mother said a simple promissory note from Paul was sufficient, and she would have her attorney draft the note.

The attorney drafted the note but was concerned about the inequity: "You never made a Will. Were you to die, each of your children stands to inherit an equal amount of money. All of the money you gave to Frank will not count towards his inheritance unless you make a Will saying that amount must be subtracted from his inheritance, or unless he gives you a promissory note. If Paul still owes money on this promissory note, he will either need to pay the balance to your Estate, or have it subtracted from the amount he inherits. If you make a Will you can adjust for monies borrowed by Paul and monies that you gave to Frank" (MN 524.2-109).

"It's O.K." replied the woman "I love all my children equally . . . some a little more equal than others."

📑 SET THE PERSONAL REPRESENTATIVE'S FEE

An important reason to make a Will is so that you can choose your Personal Representative and come to an understanding about how much compensation he/she is to receive. You can state that value in your Will.

 THE PERSONAL REPRESENTATIVE
CAN SEEK MORE MONEY

Even though your Will states the amount of compensation to be given to your Personal Representative, he may decide to ask the Probate Court to award a greater value. Under Minnesota law, unless the Personal Representative signed an agreement, he has the right to refuse the amount stated in the Will and ask the Court to award his a fee based on the following:

⇨   the time and labor required to settle the Estate

⇨   the complexity and novelty of problems involved

⇨   the extent of his responsibilities (the size of the Estate) and the results obtained (MN 524.3-719).

If this is of concern to you, have your attorney draft a fee agreement for your Personal Representative and attach it to your Will. By signing the Agreement, your Personal Representative is promising to accept the fee as provided in the Will.

You also need to keep in mind that the Personal Representative's fee is just to administer the Estate. It does not include payment for professional work he may do while administering the Estate. For example, if you appoint your attorney as Personal Representative, he can agree to the amount stated in the Will for his role as Personal Representative and then ask the Court to award him additional compensation for the performance of his duties as attorney for the Estate.

The same goes for any professional. If you chose an accountant to be your Personal Representative, he can ask to be compensated for his role as Personal Representative and also for any accounting work that he performs while settling the Estate.

📑 CHOOSE A GUARDIAN FOR A MINOR CHILD

Each parent has the right to name someone in their Will to be Guardian of their child in the event that the parent dies before the child is grown, and the other parent is deceased. Should the surviving parent die, then whoever the parent named to serve as Guardian will have priority to be appointed as guardian of the minor child. If the child is 14 or older, the Court will give priority to the child's choice of guardian, unless the Court finds that it is not in the child's best interest to appoint that person (MN 525.615, 525.616).

📑 INCLUDE SAFEGUARDS FOR YOUR BENEFICIARIES

It is fairly common practice in Minnesota to include a waiver in the Will directing that the Personal Representative be allowed to conduct the Probate procedure without Court supervision. The Will maker may include the waiver because he is trying to make the job easier for his Personal Representative; or maybe he is concerned with the cost of the Probate procedure. But as explained on page 145, the main difference between a Supervised and an Unsupervised Probate proceeding is that with an Unsupervised proceeding the Personal Representative can close the Estate and distribute the property without Court approval.

With a Supervised Probate proceeding, your beneficiaries can raise any concern they have about the way the Probate was conducted, or about the way the Personal Representative intends to distribute the property. The Court will conduct a hearing on the matter. The Estate will not be closed until all of the issues are resolved.

There is no such safeguard if your Will directs that the Probate proceeding be unsupervised. And as explained on page 148, your beneficiary could request that the Probate be Supervised, but the Court won't grant the request unless the beneficiary can prove that there is some danger of loss.

THE BENEFICIARY CAN SIGN HIS OWN WAIVER

Some Will makers may want their Personal Representative to have sole authority in the Probate proceeding. They see no need to have input from the beneficiaries during the Estate Administration. That is often the case with a married couple. Each names the other to be Personal Representative and sole beneficiary of the Estate. But suppose the couple die simultaneously in a car accident. Would the Will maker have wanted the alternate Personal Representative to have such authority over the beneficiaries of the Estate?

The thing to keep in mind, is that once you include a waiver in your Will, you are taking a right away from your beneficiary. If you waive Court supervision you are in effect, taking away your beneficiary's right to the safeguard of a Court review of the Probate proceeding before the Estate is closed.

The beneficiary is always free to sign his own waiver. If your beneficiary is satisfied with the way things were done, he can always sign a waiver approving the proposed distribution and the closing of the Estate.

PREPARING AND STORING YOUR WILL

Some people think that a Will is a simple thing — something they can do themselves. But preparing a Will is like figure skating. It is harder than it looks. A Will needs to be clearly worded. A sentence that can be read in two different ways can lead to a dispute over what you intended; and that could result in a long and expensive Court battle. The Will must be signed and witnessed according to Minnesota law, otherwise the Judge may refuse to admit the Will to Probate, and your property will be distributed as if you had no Will at all.

Unless you take the time to make yourself knowledgable about Minnesota law as it relates to Wills, it is best to have an attorney who is experienced in Estate Planning, prepare one for you.

STORING THE WILL

Once you sign your Will, you may wonder where to store it. Your attorney may suggest that he place it in his vault for safekeeping. By doing so, he ensures that your heirs will need to contact him as soon as you die. This does not mean that they are required to employ him should a Probate proceeding be necessary. It only means that he will have an opportunity for future employment. In exchange, he gives you a good value. Your Will is kept safely in his vault, and at sole cost to him.

Before allowing your attorney to store the Will, you need assurance that the attorney will be responsible for the document. You should get a receipt and something in writing that says:

⇨ The attorney accepts full responsibility for the storage of the Will. Should it be lost or damaged, he will replace the document at no cost to you; and if you are deceased, he will, at no cost to your heirs, present sufficient evidence to the Court to accept a valid copy of the Will into Probate.

⇨ There will be no charge to you, or your heirs, for the storage and retrieval of the document.

With all of this cost and liability, many attorneys will agree only to store a copy of your Will. In such case, you can keep the document in a fireproof safe deposit box within your home; and give a duplicate key to the person you have chosen to be your Personal Representative.

THE SAFE DEPOSIT BOX — SAFE BUT . . .

You might consider placing your document in a safe deposit box that you lease from a bank or other financial institution. The only problem with the bank safe deposit box is convenient access.

As explained on page 78, if you hold a safe deposit box in your name only, access to the box is restricted once you die. The bank will not allow anyone to enter your safe deposit box unless they sign an Affidavit, and a company employee is present when they enter the safe deposit box (MN 55.10). If your next of kin cannot locate the key to your safe deposit box, it may be necessary to have a Personal Representative appointed in order to get the contents of the box.

LEASE THE BOX JOINTLY WITH ANOTHER

You could lease a safe deposit box jointly with your spouse or a trusted family member, each of you with the right to enter the safe deposit box. Should you die, your spouse, or joint lessee can go to the safe deposit box and remove your Will and any other item in the box.

Regardless of where you choose to store your Will, let your Personal Representative know that you have a Will and how to retrieve it in the event of your death.

CHOOSING THE RIGHT ESTATE PLAN

Joint Ownership?
A POD Account?
A TOD Security?
A Trust?
A Will?
An Insurance Policy???

Chapters 7 and 8 offer so many options that the reader may be more confused than when he was blissfully unenlightened.

As with most things in life, you may find there are no ultimate solutions, just alternatives. The right choice for you is the one that best accomplishes your goal. This being the case, you first need to determine what you want to accomplish with the money you leave. Think about what will happen to your property if you were to die suddenly, without making any plan different from the one you now have.

     Who will be responsible to pay your bills?
     Who will get your property?
     Will Probate be necessary?

If the answers to these questions are not what you wish, then you need to work to arrange your property to accomplish your goals.

For those with significant assets, — especially those with Estates large enough to pay Estate taxes, a trip to an experienced Estate Planning attorney may be well worth the consultation fee.

Your Estate Plan Record   9

Once you are satisfied with your Estate Plan, then the final thing to consider is whether your heirs will be able to locate your assets once you are deceased.

Most people have their business records in one place, their Will in another place, car titles and deeds in still another place. When someone dies, their beneficiaries may feel as if they are playing a game of "hide and seek" with the decedent. The game might be fun were it not for the fact that an unlocated item may be forever lost. For example, suppose you die in an accident and no one knows you are insured by your credit card company for accidental death in the amount of $25,000. The only one to profit is the insurance company, which is just that much richer because no one told them that you died as a result of an accident.

And how about a key to a safe deposit box located in another state? Will anyone find it? Even if they find the key, how will they find the box?

It is not difficult to arrange things so that your affairs are always in order. It amounts to being aware of what you own (and owe) and keeping a record of your possessions. A side benefit is that by doing so, you will always know where all your business records are. If you ever spent time trying to collect information to file your taxes or trying to find a lost stock or bond certificate, you will appreciate the value of organizing your records.

ORGANIZING YOUR RECORDS

Heirs need all the help they can get. It is difficult enough dealing with the loss, without the frustration of trying to locate important documents. Your heirs will have no problem locating your assets if you keep all of your records in a single place. It can be a desk drawer or a file cabinet or even a shoe box. It is helpful if you keep a separate file or folder for each type of investment. You might consider setting up the following folders:

📁 **THE BANK & SECURITIES FOLDER**

Store your original certificates for stocks, bonds, mutual funds, certificates of deposit, in a folder labeled **BANK & SECURITIES FOLDER**. In addition to the original certificate include a copy of the contract you signed with each financial institution. The contract will show where you have funds and who you named as beneficiary or joint owner of the account. If someone owes you money and has signed a promissory note or mortgage that identifies you as the lender, then you can store these documents in this folder as well.

If you wish to store your original documents in a safe deposit box, then keep a record of the location of the safe deposit box, and the number of the box, in this folder. Make a copy of all of the items stored in the box and place the copies in this folder. If you have an extra key to the box, then put the key in the folder. If you are the only person with access to the box, it may take a Probate proceeding to remove items from the box once you die. Consider allowing someone you trust to be able to gain entry to the box in the event of your incapacity or death.

📁 THE INSURANCE FOLDER

The **INSURANCE FOLDER** is for each original insurance policy that you own, be it life insurance, car insurance, homeowner's insurance or health care insurance. If you purchased real property, you may have received a title commitment to insure title to the property at closing. If so, you should have received the title insurance policy some weeks later when you received your original deed from recording. If you cannot find the title insurance policy, contact the closing agent and have them send you a copy of your title policy.

📁 THE PENSION AND ANNUITY FOLDER

If you have a Pension or Annuity, then put all of the documents relating to the Pension in this folder. Include the telephone number and/or address of the person to contact in the event of your death.

FOR FEDERAL RETIREES If you are a Federal Retiree, you should have received your **PERSONAL IDENTIFICATION NUMBER (PIN)** and the person who will inherit your pension (your *survivor annuitant*) should have received his/her own PIN as well. It is relatively simple to obtain this during your lifetime, but it may be difficult and/or stressful for your survivor annuitant to work through the system once you are gone.

Survivor annuitant benefits are not automatic. Your survivor annuitant must apply for them by submitting a death claim to the Office of Personnel Management. Your survivor needs to know that it is necessary to apply and also how to apply. You can get printed information about how apply for benefits from the Office Of Personnel Management (see Page 32). Keep the printed information in this file.

🗁 THE DEED FOLDER

Many people save every scrap of paper associated with the closing of real property. If you closed recently on real estate and there was a mortgage involved in the purchase, you probably walked away from closing with enough paper to wallpaper your kitchen. If you wish, you can keep all of those papers in a separate file that identifies the property, for example:

CLOSING PAPERS FOR THE ST. PAUL PROPERTY

Place the original deed (or a copy if the original is in a safe deposit box) in a separate **DEED FOLDER**. Include cemetery deeds, condominium deeds, cooperative shares to real property, timesharing certificates, deed to out of state property, etc. Also include a copy of related documents such as an Abstract of Title, or a recorded Condominium Approval. If you have a title insurance policy, put the original in the insurance folder, and a copy in this folder. If you have a mortgage on your property, put a copy of the recorded mortgage and promissory note in a separate **LIABILITY FOLDER**.

LOCATING REAL PROPERTY

If you own a vacant lot, your beneficiaries will find the deed (or a copy) in this folder but that deed will not contain the address of that property because it doesn't have one. The post office does not assign a street address until someone actually lives at the site. Your beneficiary could get the location of the property from city or county records. But why make things hard for them? Include a simple handwritten note in this folder that tells them exactly how to locate the property.

THE LIABILITY FOLDER

The LIABILITY FOLDER should contain all loan documents of debts that you owe. For example, if you purchased real property and have a mortgage on that property, put a copy of the mortgage and promissory note in this folder. If you owe money on a car, put the loan documents in this folder. If you have a credit card, put a copy of the contract you signed with the credit card company in this folder.

Many people never take the time to calculate their net worth (what a person owns less what that person owes). By having a record of your assets and outstanding debts, you can calculate your net worth whenever you wish.

THE ESTATE PLANNING DOCUMENT FOLDER

Place your Will and/or Trust in a separate folder. If your attorney has your original Will, then make a note of that fact together with a copy of the Will. If the original document is in a safe deposit box, then place a copy of the document in this folder together with instructions about how to find the original.

It is important to keep a copy of your Will or Trust because over the years you may forget what provision you made. Keeping a copy in your home may save you a trip to the safe deposit box to determine whether you need to update the document.

THE PERSONAL PROPERTY FOLDER

MOTOR VEHICLES

Put all motor vehicle titles in a Personal Property folder. This includes cars, mobile homes, boats, planes, etc. If you owe money on the vehicle, the lender may have possession of the title certificate. If such is the case, then put a copy of the title certificate and registration in this folder and a copy of the loan documents in a separate liability folder. If you have a boat or plane, then identify the location of the motor vehicle. For example, if you are leasing space in an airplane hangar or in a marina, keep a copy of the leasing agreement in this file.

JEWELRY

If you own expensive jewelry, keep a picture of the item together with the sales receipt or written appraisal in this folder.

COLLECTOR'S ITEMS

If you own a valuable art or coin collection, or any other item of significant value, include a picture of the item in this file. Also include evidence of ownership of the item, such as a sales receipt or a certificate of authenticity, or a written appraisal of the property.

THE PERSONAL RECORDS FOLDER

The **PERSONAL RECORDS FOLDER** should include documents that relate to you personally, such as a birth certificate, naturalization papers, pre-nuptial or post- nuptial agreement, marriage certificate, divorce papers, military records, social security card; etc. If you have a Power of Attorney or a Health Care Directive, then this is a good place for these documents. If you placed the original document in a safe deposit box, then keep a copy in this folder together with the location of the original.

THE TAX RECORD FOLDER

Your Personal Representative (or next of kin) will need to file your final income tax returns. Keep a copy of your tax returns (both federal and state) for the past three years in your Tax Record Folder.

As explained in Chapter 2, beginning in 2010, there will be a cap on the step-up basis to 4.3 million dollars for property inherited by the spouse and 1.3 million dollars for property inherited by anyone else. It is important to keep a record of the basis of your property, not only for your heirs, but yourself should you decide to sell the property during your lifetime. If you purchase real property, you need to keep a record of the purchase price as well as monies you paid to improve the property. You will need these records to determine whether there will be a Capital Gains Tax on the transfer. Your accountant can help you set up a bookkeeping system to keep a running record of your basis in everything you own of value.

THE *If I Die* FILE

Many do not have the time, nor inclination, to "play" with all these folders. They do not anticipate an immediate demise. Getting hit by a truck, or dying in a fiery plane crash is not something to think about, much less prepare for. But consider that death is not the only problem. You could take suddenly ill (say with a stroke) and become incapacitated. Even the most time-starved optimist should have a murmur of concern that his loved ones will be left with a mess should something unforeseen happen.

If you do not feel like doing a complete job of organizing your records at this time, consider an abridged version. You can set up a single file with a list of all you own and the location of each item. You need to make that file easily accessible to whoever you wish to manage your affairs in the event of your incapacity or death. You can do this by letting that person know of the existence of the file and how to get it in an emergency; or keep the file in an easily accessed place in your home with the succinct but attention-grabbing title of "*If I Die*."

We have included a form on the next page that you can use as a basis for information to be included in the file.

If I Die

then the following information will help settle my estate:

INFORMATION FOR DEATH CERTIFICATE

MY FULL LEGAL NAME _____

MY SOCIAL SECURITY NO. _____

MY USUAL OCCUPATION _____

BIRTH DATE AND BIRTH PLACE _____

If naturalized, date & place _____

MY FATHER'S NAME _____

MY MOTHER'S MAIDEN NAME _____

PERSONS TO BE NOTIFIED OF MY DEATH

_____

_____

_____

FUNERAL AND BURIAL ARRANGEMENTS

LOCATION OF BURIAL SITE

_____

LOCATION OF PREPAID FUNERAL CONTRACT

_____

FOR VETERAN or SPOUSE BURIAL IN A NATIONAL CEMETERY

BRANCH_____SERIAL NO._____

VETERAN'S RANK _____

VETERAN'S VA CLAIM NUMBER _____

DATE AND PLACE OF ENTRY INTO SERVICE:

_____

DATE AND PLACE OF SEPARATION FROM SERVICE:

_____

LOCATION OF OFFICIAL MILITARY DISCHARGE
OR DD 214 FORM_____

LOCATION OF LEGAL DOCUMENTS

BIRTH CERTIFICATE _____

MARRIAGE CERTIFICATE_____

DIVORCE DECREE _____

PASSPORT _____

WILL OR TRUST _____

DEEDS _____

MORTGAGES _____

TITLE TO MOTOR VEHICLES _____

HEALTH CARE DIRECTIVES _____

Name, telephone of attorney _____

LOCATION OF FINANCIAL RECORDS

INSURANCE POLICIES:

Name of Company, Location of Policy, Insurance Agent

_____

_____

PENSIONS/ANNUITIES:

IF FEDERAL RETIREE: PIN NUMBER: _____

NAME OF SURVIVOR _____

SURVIVOR PIN NUMBER _____

BANK

Name and address of Bank, Account Number,
Location of Safe Deposit Box and Key

_____

_____

SECURITIES

Name and telephone number of broker

_____

TAX RECORDS FOR PAST 3 YEARS

LOCATION _____

Name and telephone number of accountant

_____

WHEN TO UPDATE YOUR ESTATE PLAN

We discussed people's natural disinclination to make an Estate Plan until they are faced with their own mortality. Many believe that they will make just one Will and then die (maybe that's why they put off making a Will). The reality is, most people who make a Will change it at least once before they die. If you have an Estate Plan, it is important to update it when any of the following events take place:

✍ A CHANGE IN RELATIONSHIP

If you marry, divorce, have a child, or if a beneficiary of your Estate dies, you need to examine your Estate Plan to determine whether it needs to be revised. If you decide that your Will needs a complete revision, then it is important to have a new Will prepared. If you simply rip up the old Will, that will effectively revoke the Will. But it could happen that someone (perhaps your attorney) has a copy of the Will. If no one knows that you revoked the Will, they may think the Will is lost and then offer the copy of the Will for Probate (see page 74). If you draft a new Will, then the first paragraph should say, "I revoke all prior Wills ..."

BENEFICIARY MOVES OR DIES: Most of us remember to name an alternate beneficiary should a beneficiary die during ones lifetime. But how many of us remember to notify the pension plan or insurance company of a change of address? It is important that your beneficiary's address be available to those in charge of distributing funds upon your death. Many insurance policies are never paid because the company cannot locate the beneficiary. In 1998, the Office of Federal Employees' Group Life Insurance reported that they had 29 million dollars in unpaid benefits, mostly because the beneficiary could not be located at their last given address.

✍ CHANGE IN MARITAL STATUS

Under Minnesota law, should you divorce and then die before you get around to changing your Will, any gift that you made in your Will or Trust for your former spouse is revoked. Your Probate Estate will be distributed as if your spouse died before you did. A legal separation in the state of Minnesota does not end the marriage, so these laws do not apply to couples who are separated, legally, or otherwise (MN 501B.90, 524.2-804). If you divorce (or even separate) it is important to review all of your Estate Planning documents (deeds, pension plans, insurance policies, Will or Trust etc.) to determine whether you wish to name a new beneficiary of your property.

NOTIFY EMPLOYER OF CHANGE IN RELATIONSHIP

If you change your marital status (either marry or divorce) you need to tell your employer of the change so that the employer can change your status for purposes of pay check withdrawals and health insurance coverage.

✍ RELOCATION TO A NEW STATE OR COUNTRY

There is no need to change your Estate Plan for a move within the state of Minnesota. If you deposited your Will with the Probate Court, you need to retrieve it and then deposit your Will in the Probate Court of the county of your new residence (MN 524.2-515).

If you move out of state, you need to determine whether your Will conforms to the laws of that state. Most states will honor a Will drafted according to Minnesota law, however, the rights of a spouse vary considerably state to state.

If you are married and have not provided for your spouse according to the laws of that state, your Will may be challenged, on that basis. The rights of a spouse to inherit property varies significantly from state to state. There is a world of difference between the rights of a spouse in a community property state and other states. And there is even variation in the rights of a spouse from one community property state to another.

If you are married and have a Will or Trust, you need to check with an attorney to be sure that your Will or Trust cannot be challenged in the new state because you did not leave your spouse the minimum amount required by the laws of that state.

If you do not have a Will, then it is important to check out the Laws of Intestate Succession for that state. Each state (and country) has its own laws relating to the inheritance of property and those laws are very different from each other. Who has the right to inherit your property in the state of Minnesota may be different from who can inherit your property in another state. If you do not have a Will, then this is the time to think about who will get your property in the state of your new residence.

You also need to check out the taxes of the new state. Each state has its own tax structure. Some states have an inheritance tax, or a transfer tax on all inherited property. If state taxes are high, you may need an Estate Plan that will minimize the impact of those taxes.

Creditor protection is another item that is significantly different state to state. If you have much debt, then determine what items can be inherited by your family free of your debts.

OTHER ESTATE PLANNING DOCUMENTS

If you have appointed someone to handle your finances under a Power of Attorney or make your medical decisions under a Health Care Directive you need to determine whether these documents will be honored in the new state.

Laws relating to health care vary significantly. Other states may not have laws providing for the appointment of a Health Care Agent, but they may have laws that enable you to appoint a Patient Advocate or a Health Care Surrogate who can make your health care decisions should you be too ill to do so yourself. It is best to sign a new document using the form and terminology recognized in that state, rather than chance any confusion should you become ill and find yourself in an emergency situation.

When moving to another state you need to either educate yourself about the laws of the state, or consult with an attorney who can assist you in reviewing your Estate Plan to see if that plan will accomplish your goals in that state.

✎ A SIGNIFICANT CHANGE IN THE LAW

We pay our legislators (state and federal) to make laws and, if necessary, change those in effect. We pay judges to interpret the law and that interpretation may change the way the law operates. The legislature and the judiciary do their job and so laws change frequently. Tax laws are particularly volatile. The 2001 change in the Federal Estate Tax law gradually increases the Exclusion amount so that by 2010 no Federal Estate Tax will be due regardless of the value of your Estate. You may be thinking that there is no need for an Estate Tax plan because you don't intend to die prior to 2010. But any certainty relating to death and taxes is false security (especially taxes, in this case). As explained in Chapter 2, the law as passed in 2001, is effective only until December 31, 2010. If lawmakers do nothing, then on January 1, 2011, the Federal Estate Tax goes back into effect; and Estates that exceed one million dollars will once again be subject to Estate taxes.

And that is not the only uncertainty. Each state has its own Estate Tax structure. It remains to be seen how each state will react to the federal change. Some states may follow the lead of the federal government and increase their Estate Tax Exclusion in the same manner. Other states may see this as an opportunity to "pick up the slack" i.e., to increase their Estate Taxes, so that monies that would have been paid to the federal government will now be paid to the state.

You need to keep up with the news to learn about changes in the law that affect your Estate Plan. It is a good idea to check with your attorney on a regular basis to see if any change in the state or federal law affects your current Estate plan. And also check out the Eagle Publishing Company Web site for changes we will post to keep this book fresh. http://www.eaglepublishing.com

GAMES DECEDENTS PLAY

We discussed the game of "hide and seek" some decedents play with their heirs. A variation of that game is the "wild goose chase." The person who plays this game is one who never updates his files. His records are filled with all sorts of lapsed insurance policies, promissory notes of debts long since paid; brokerage statements of securities that have been sold, and so on.

When he is gone, his family will become frustrated as they try to hunt down the "missing" asset. If you wish to play this game, then the best joke is to keep the key to a safe deposit box that you are no longer leasing. That will keep folks hunting for a long time!

If you do not have a wicked sense of humor, then do your family a favor and update your records on a regular basis.

Glossary

ABSTRACT OF TITLE   An *Abstract of Title* is a condensed history of the title to the land, consisting of a summary of all of documents recorded with the County Recorder that affect the land, including mortgages and contracts for deed.

ADMINISTRATION The *administration* of a Probate Estate is the management and settlement of the decedent's affairs. There are different types of administration. See *ancillary administration*.

AFFIANT   An *affiant* is someone who signs an affidavit and swears or acknowledges that it is true in the presence of a notary public or other person with authority to administer an oath or take acknowledgments.

AFFIDAVIT   An *affidavit* is a written statement of fact made by someone voluntarily, under oath, or acknowledged as being true, in the presence of a notary public or someone else who has authority to administer an oath or take acknowledgments.

AGENT   An *Agent* is someone who is authorized by another (the principal) to act for or in place of the principal.

ANATOMICAL GIFT   An *anatomical gift* is the donation of all or part of the body of the decedent for a specified purpose, such as transplantation or research.

ANCILLARY ADMINISTRATION An *ancillary administration* is a probate procedure that aids or assists the original (primary) probate proceeding. Ancillary administration is conducted in another state to determine the beneficiary of the decedent's property located within that state, and to determine whether the property is taxable in that state.

ANNUITANT   An *annuitant* is someone who is entitled to receive payments under an annuity contract.

ANNUITY An *annuity* is a contract that gives someone (the annuitant) the right to receive periodic payments (monthly, quarterly) either for life or for a number of years.

ASSET An *asset* is anything owned by someone that has a value, including personal property (jewelry, paintings, securities, cash, motor vehicles, etc.) and real property (condominiums, vacant lots, acreage, residences, etc.)

BASIS   The *basis* is a value that is assigned to an asset for the purpose of determining the gain (or loss) on the sale of the item or in determining the value of the item in the hands of someone who has received it as a gift.

BENEFICIARY A *beneficiary* is one who benefits from the act of another or from the transfer of property. In this book we refer to a beneficiary as someone named in a Will or Trust to receive property, or someone who inherits property under the Laws of Intestate Succession.

BY REPRESENTATION   *By Representation* is a method of distributing property to a group of people such that if one of them dies before the gift is made, the deceased person's share goes to his/her descendants.

CAPITAL GAINS TAX A *Capital Gains tax* is a tax on the increase in the basis of property sold by a taxpayer.

CAVEAT *Caveat* is Latin for "Let him beware." It is a warning for the reader to be careful.

CERTIFICATE OF TITLE A *Certificate of Title* is a document that is prepared and recorded by the Registrar of Titles in the county where the property is located. The Certificate identifies the legal description of the property and the identity of the current owner.

CHARITABLE REMAINDER ANNUITY TRUST   A *Charitable Remainder Annuity Trust* is a Trust that is required to pay an annuity to a designated person for a certain period of time. Once the annuity is paid, whatever remains in the Trust is donated to a tax exempt charity.

CLAIM A *claim* against the decedent's estate is a demand for payment of a debt of the decedent. To be effective, the claim must be filed with the Probate court within the time limits set by law.

CODE   A *Code* is a body of laws arranged systematically for easy reference e.g. the Internal Revenue Code.

COLUMBARIUM A *Columbarium* is a vault with niches (spaces) for urns that contain the ashes of cremated bodies.

COMMISSIONER A *Commissioner* is someone appointed by the Court or by the government to do a job.

COMMON LAW MARRIAGE   A *Common Law marriage* is one that is entered into without a state marriage license nor any kind of official marriage ceremony. A common law marriage is created by an agreement to marry, followed by the two living together as man and wife. Most states do not recognize a common law marriage.

CONSERVATOR   A *Conservator* is someone appointed by the Probate Court to manage, protect and preserve the property of someone who is missing, or who the Court finds is unable to care for his property because of age (a minor) or incapacity.

CONTRACT FOR DEED A *Contract for Deed* is essentially a mortgage. The seller of the property agrees to transfer title to the property (the deed) to the buyer once the buyer pays the amount agreed upon.

COURT The *Court* as used in this book is the Probate Court. When referring to an order made by the court then the term is synonymous with "judge," i.e., an "order of the court" is an order made by the judge of the court.

CREMAINS The word *Cremains* is an abbreviation of the term *cremated remains*. It is also referred to as the *ashes* of a person who has been cremated.

CUSTODIAN A *Custodian* under the *Uniform Transfers to Minors Act* is a person or a financial institution that accepts responsibility for the care and management of property given to a minor child.

DAMAGES *Damages* is money that is awarded by a Court as compensation to someone who has been injured by the action of another.

DECEDENT The *Decedent* is the person who died.

DESCENDANT A *descendant* is someone who descends from a common ancestor. There are two kinds of descendants: a *lineal descendant* and a *collateral descendant*. The lineal descendant is one who descends in a straight line such as father to son to grandson. The collateral descendant is one who descends in a parallel line, such as a cousin. In this book, unless otherwise stated, the term *descendant* refers to a *lineal descendant*.

DEVISEE A *Devisee* is someone who inherits a gift of real property by Will.

DISTRIBUTION The *distribution* of a Trust Estate or a Probate Estate is the transfer to a beneficiary of that part of the estate to which the beneficiary is entitled.

DURABLE POWER OF ATTORNEY A *Durable Power of Attorney* is a document in which the person who signs the document (the *Principal*) gives another person (his *Attorney in Fact*) authority to do certain things on behalf of the Principal. The Attorney in Fact is also referred to as the Principal's *Agent*. The word "*durable*" means that the authority of the Agent continues even if the Principal is incapacitated at the time that the Agent is acting on behalf of the Principal.

ELECTIVE SHARE The *Elective Share* is the minimum amount of the decedent's estate that a surviving spouse is entitled to receive under the law.

ENCUMBRANCE An *encumbrance* is a claim or a lien or a liability that is attached to real property, such as a mortgage, lease, or mechanic's lien.

EQUITABLE *Equitable* is whatever is right or just. If property is distributed to two or more people equitably, then the division is not necessarily equal, but according to the principles of justice or fairness.

ESTATE A person's *Estate* is all of the property (both real and personal property) owned by that person. The decedent's estate may also be referred to as his *Taxable Estate* because all of the decedent's assets must be included when determining whether any Estate taxes are due after the person dies. Compare to Probate Estate.

EXECUTOR An *Executor* is someone appointed by a Will maker to carry out instructions made in the Will, and to dispose of the Will maker's property in the manner described in the Will. In Minnesota, Executors are referred to as Personal Representatives.

FIDUCIARY A *Fiduciary* is one who holds property in trust for another or one who acts for the benefit of another, such as a Personal Representative, trustee, guardian, conservator, etc.

GRANTEE The *Grantee* named in a deed is the person who receives title to the property from the Grantor.

GRANTOR A *Grantor* is someone who transfers property. The grantor of a deed is the person who transfers property to a new owner (the *Grantee*). The grantor of a trust is someone who creates the trust and then transfer's property into the trust. See *Settlor*.

GUARDIAN A *Guardian* is someone who has legal authority to care for the person and/or property of a minor or for someone who has been found by the court to be incapacitated.

HEALTH CARE AGENT A *Health Care Agent* is someone who is appointed by another (the *Principal)* to make medical decisions on behalf of the Principal, in the event that the Principal is to too ill to speak for himself.

HEALTH CARE DIRECTIVE A *Health Care Directive* is a statement made by someone (the principal) in the presence of witnesses or a written, notarized statement in which the principal gives directions about the health care he/she wishes to receive. See *Living Will*.

HOMESTEAD The *homestead* is the dwelling and land owned and occupied as the owner's principal residence.

HEIR An *heir* is anyone entitled to inherit the decedent's property under the Laws of Descent and Distribution in the event that the decedent dies without a Will.

INCAPACITATED The term *incapacitated* is used in two ways. A person is *physically incapacitated* if he lacks the strength or dexterity to care for himself in some way. A person is *legally incapacitated* if a court finds that a person is unable to care for his person or property. Once the Court determines that a person is legally incapacitated, the judge will appoint someone to care for the person and/or property of the incapacitated person.

INDIGENT A person who is *indigent* is one who is poor and without funds.

INSOLVENT A person or business is *insolvent* if more money is owed than owned, or if the person or business is unable to pay debts as they come due.

INTER VIVOS TRUST An *Inter Vivos Trust* (also known as a *Living Trust*) is a Trust that is created and becomes effective during the lifetime of the Settlor (or Grantor) as contrasted with a Trust that the Settlor includes as part of his Will to take effect upon his death.

INTESTATE *Intestate* means not having a Will or dying without a Will. *Testate* is to have a Will or dying with a Will.

ISSUE The decedent's *issue* is his direct or lineal descendant, child, grandchild, etc. See Descendant.

JOINT AND SEVERAL LIABILITY   If two or more people agree to be *jointly and severally liable* to pay a debt, then each individually agrees to be responsible to pay the entire debt, and together they all agree to pay for the debt.

JOINT TENANCY   In Minnesota, a *Joint Tenancy* means that each of tenant owns an equal share of the property with right of survivorship; i.e., should one Joint Tenant die the remaining tenants own the property.

KEY MAN INSURANCE   *Key man insurance* is an insurance policy designed to protect a company from economic loss in the event that an important employee of the company becomes disabled or dies.

LEGALESE   *Legalese* refers to the use of legal terms and confusing text that is used by some attorneys to draft legal documents.

LETTERS *Letters* is a document, issued by the Probate court, giving the Personal Representative authority to take possession of and to administer the estate of the decedent.

LIEN   A *lien* is a charge against a person's property as security for a debt. The lien is evidence of the creditor's right to take the property as full or partial payment, in the event that the debtor defaults in paying the monies owed.

LIFE ESTATE A *Life Estate* interest in real property is the right to possess and occupy that property for so long as the holder of the Life Estate lives.

LITIGATION *Litigation* is the process of carrying on a lawsuit, i.e., to sue for some right or remedy in a court of law. A Litigation Attorney is one who is experienced in conducting the law suit and in particular, going to trial.

LIVING WILL   A *Living Will* is a Health Care Directive that gives instructions about whether life support systems should be withheld in the event that the person who signs the Living Will is terminally ill or in a persistent vegetative state and unable to speak for himself.

MEDICAID *Medicaid* is a public assistance program sponsored jointly by the federal and state government to provide medical care for people with few assets and low income. In Minnesota the program is known as *Medical Assistance*.

NET PROBATE ESTATE The *Net Probate Estate* is the value of the decedent's Probate Estate, less all the monies paid to settle the Estate, i.e. what is left once all valid claims and the costs and expenses of the Probate proceedings are paid.

NET PROCEEDS The *net proceeds* of a sale is the sale price less costs and expenses paid to make the sale.

NET WORTH   A person's *net worth* is the value of the property he owns less the monies he owes.

NEXT OF KIN   *Next of kin* has two meanings in law: *next of kin* can refer to a person's nearest blood relation or it can refer to those people (not necessarily blood relations) who are entitled to inherit the property of the decedent if the decedent died without a will.

PERJURY *Perjury* is lying under oath. The false statement can be made as a witness in court or by signing an Affidavit. Perjury is a criminal offense.

PERSONAL PROPERTY *Personal property* is all property owned by a person that is not real property (real estate). It includes cars, stocks, house furnishings, jewelry, etc.

PERSONAL REPRESENTATIVE A *Personal Representative* is someone who is appointed by the Probate court to settle the decedent's estate and to distribute whatever is left to the proper beneficiary.

PETITION A *Petition* is a formal written request to a Court asking the Court to take action or issue an order on a given matter.

POST-NUPTIAL AGREEMENT A *Post-nuptial agreement* is an agreement made by a couple after marriage to decide their respective rights in case of a dissolution of their marriage or the death of a spouse.

POWER OF ATTORNEY A *Power of Attorney* is a document in which the person who signs the document (the *Principal*) gives another person (his *Agent*) authority to do certain things on behalf of the Principal.

PRE-NUPTIAL AGREEMENT A *Pre-nuptial agreement* (also known as an *Antenuptial agreement*) is an agreement made prior to marriage whereby a couple determines how their property is to be managed during their marriage and how their property is to be divided should one die, or they later divorce.

PRESENT VALUE   The *present value* is the current value of a future payment, or series of payments, discounted at a certain rate. To compute that value you would need to know the period of time the money will come due and the discount rate to be applied.

PRINCIPAL In a Power of Attorney, the *Principal* is the person who permits or directs another to act for him.

PROBATE   *Probate* is a court proceeding in which a court determines the existence of a valid Will and then supervises the distribution of the Probate Estate of the decedent.

PROBATE ESTATE   The *Probate Estate* is that part of the decedent's estate that is subject to probate. It includes property that the decedent owned in his name only. It does not include property that was jointly held by the decedent and someone else. It does not include property held "in trust for" or "for the benefit of" someone.

PUNITIVE DAMAGES   *Punitive damages* are awarded by a Court to punish someone who deliberately disregarded the rights or safety of another (MN 549.20). It is money awarded in addition to *compensatory damages* which are monies awarded to reimburse the wronged person for actual losses.

REAL PROPERTY   *Real property,* also known as *real estate,* is land and anything permanently attached to the land such as buildings and fences.

REGISTERED AGENT   A *Registered Agent* of a corporation is someone who is authorized to act on behalf of the company and accept service of process in the event the company is sued.

RECEIVER A *Receiver* is a person appointed by a Court to take possession of property whenever there is a danger that in the absence of such appointment, the property will be lost or removed. The Receiver acts as a Trustee preserving and managing the property according to Court order.

RESIDUARY BENEFICIARY A *residuary beneficiary* of a Will is a beneficiary who is entitled to whatever is left of the Probate Estate once the specific gifts made in the Will have been distributed and once the decedent's bills, taxes and costs of probate have been paid. If there is more than one residuary beneficiary, then they share equally in the residuary estate.

RESIDUARY ESTATE A *Residuary Estate* is that part of a probate estate that is left after all expenses and costs of administration have been paid and specific gifts have been distributed.

REVOCABLE LIVING TRUST A *Revocable Living Trust* (also known as an *Inter Vivos Trust*) is Trust that is created and becomes effective during the lifetime of the Grantor as contrasted with a Trust that the Grantor includes as part of his Will to take effective upon his death. A revocable Trust is one that can be changed or cancelled at any time by the Grantor.

SETTLOR A *Settlor* or *Trustor* is someone who creates a Trust.

SOLEMNIZE To *solemnize* a marriage is to enter a marriage publicly, before witnesses, rather than privately as in a common law marriage.

SPENDTHRIFT A *spendthrift* is someone who spends money carelessly or wastefully or extravagantly.

SPENDTHRIFT TRUST   A ***Spendthrift Trust*** is a trust created to provide monies to a beneficiary, and at the same time protect the beneficiary from the monies from being taken by the his creditors.

STATUTE OF LIMITATION A ***Statute of Limitation*** is a federal or state law that sets maximum time periods for taking legal action. Once the time set out in the statute passes, no legal action can be taken.

STEP-UP BASIS   A ***step-up basis*** is the value placed on property that is acquired in a taxable transaction (such as inheriting property) or in a purchase (IRC 1012). The "step-up" refers to the increase in value of basis, from the basis of former owner (usually what he paid for it), to the basis of the new owner (usually the market value when the transfer is made).

SURROGATE   A ***surrogate*** is a substitute; someone who acts in place of another.

TENANCY BY THE ENTIRETY   A ***Tenancy by the Entirety*** is the name of a form of ownership of real property held by a husband and wife. In most states, it is equivalent to a Joint Tenancy With Right of Survivorship. There is no Tenancy by the Entirety in the state of Minnesota.

TENANCY IN COMMON   ***Tenancy in common*** is a form of ownership such that each tenant owns his/her share without any claim to that share by the other tenants. Unlike a joint tenancy, there is no right of survivorship. Once a tenant in common dies, his/her share belongs to the tenant's Estate and not to the remaining owners of the property.

TESTATE *Testate* means having made a Will or dying with a Will.

TESTATOR The *Testator* is someone who makes and signs a Will; or someone who dies leaving a Will.

TITLE INSURANCE *Title Insurance* is a policy issued by a title company after searching title to the property. The policy insures the property owner against a claim of a defective title to his property.

TORRENS TITLE SYSTEM The *Torrens title system* (named for Sir Richard Torrens) is a system for registering title to land by applying to the Court to issue a Certificate of Title.

TRUST AGREEMENT A *Trust agreement* is document in which someone (the Grantor or Trustor) creates a trust and appoints a trustee to manage property placed into the trust. The usual purpose of the trust is to benefit persons or charities named by the Grantor as beneficiaries of the trust.

TRUSTEE A *Trustee* is a person, or institution, who accepts the duty of managing property for the benefit of another.

UNDUE INFLUENCE *Undue influence* is pressure, influence or persuasion that overpowers a person's free will or judgment, so that a person acts according to the will or purpose of the dominating party.

UNSECURED CREDITOR An *unsecured creditor* is someone who is owed money on a promissory note with nothing to back it up if payment is not made. A *secured creditor* holds some special assurance of payment, such as a mortgage on real property or a lien on a car.

WAIVER   A *waiver* is the intentional and voluntary giving up of a known right.

WARRANTY DEED   A *warranty deed* is a deed in which someone (the Grantor) transfers the property to another (the Grantee) and guarantees good title, i.e., the Grantor guarantees that he has the right to transfer the property, and that no one else has any right to the property.

WRONGFUL DEATH   A *wrongful death* is a death that was caused by the willful or negligent act of a person or company.

INDEX

S

162 Minnesota Statutes are referenced in
Guiding Those Left Behind In Minnesota

Each state has its own set of laws relating to the settlement of a person's estate. The Minnesota laws that are referenced in this book are very different from the laws of other states. The author is in now in the process of "translating" *Guiding Those Left Behind* . . . for the rest of the states; that is, to write a book that incorporates the laws of the state into a book that describes how to settle the affairs of a decedent in that state, and how to prepare an Estate Plan that is appropriate for the state.

Guiding Those Left Behind is currently available for the following states:
ALABAMA, ARIZONA, CALIFORNIA, FLORIDA
GEORGIA, ILLINOIS, INDIANA, KANSAS, KENTUCKY
MASSACHUSETTS, MARYLAND, MICHIGAN
MINNESOTA, MISSOURI, MISSISSIPPI
NEW JERSEY, NEW YORK, NORTH CAROLINA, OHIO
PENNSYLVANIA, SOUTH CAROLINA, TENNESSEE
TEXAS, VIRGINIA, WASHINGTON, WISCONSIN

To check whether this book is currently available for other states:
call Eagle Publishing Company of Boca at (800) 824-0823
- or -
visit our Web site   http://www.eaglepublishing.com

BOOK REVIEWS FROM DIFFERENT STATES

ARIZONA

Ben T. Traywick of the Tombstone Epitaph said "This book is an excellent reference book that simplifies all the necessary tasks that must be done when there is a death in the family. There is even an explanation as to how you can arrange your own estate so that your heirs will not be left with a multitude of nagging problems." "The reviewer has been going through probate for two years with no end yet in sight. This book at the beginning two year ago would have helped immensely."

CALIFORNIA

Margot Petit Nichols of the Carmel Pine Cone called it a ". . .TRULY RIVETING READ." ". . . . I could scarcely put it down." "This is a book that we should all have, either on our book shelves or thoughtfully placed with our important papers."

FLORIDA

Maryhelen Clague of the Tampa Tribune Times wrote "Amelia Pohl has created a handy, self-help guide that illustrates the necessary steps that must be taken when someone dies, a guide that is easy to read, extremely clear and simple to refer to when the need arises."

NEW YORK

Saul Friedman of NEWSDAY said "And one section that should be read by readers of any age, suggests and describes how to create an 'If I Die' file to point the way to your vital papers and policies, to minimize the problems and costs for your survivors. Alas, not even you boomers will live forever."

Beyond Grief To Acceptance and Peace

AMELIA E. POHL and the noted psychologist BARBARA J. SIMMONDS, Ph.d, have written a book for those families who have suffered a loss.

Beyond Grief To Acceptance and Peace explains:
- ◇ What to say to the bereaved
- ◇ How to help a child through the loss
- ◇ Strategies to adjust to a new lifestyle
- ◇ When and where to seek assistance.

The second edition of this 80 page book is now available for $9.95 plus shipping and handling. You can order the book using the following discount coupon for a total of $9.

DISCOUNT COUPON

Please send me a copy of Beyond Grief To Acceptance and Peace

☐ I am enclosing a check for $9.
☐ Charge this to my _____ credit card
　　　　　　　　　　　(Visa, Master, etc.)

Credit Card no. _____

Expiration date: _____

Name _____

Address _____

_____

Mail this coupon to:
EAGLE PUBLISHING COMPANY OF BOCA
4199 N. Dixie Hwy. #2
Boca Raton, FL   33431

A Will is not enough in Minnesota

Many people who have a Will think that they have their affairs in order. They believe that their Will can take care of any problem that may arise. But the primary function of a Will it to distribute property to people named in a Will. A Will cannot:

⇨   Manage your personal debt

⇨   Limit your business debt

⇨   Provide care for a minor or disabled child

⇨   Appoint someone to make your health care decisions should you be unable to do so

⇨   Appoint someone to handle your finances should you be unable to do so

⇨   Arrange to pay for your health care should you need long term nursing care.

AMELIA E. POHL, ESQ. is currently writing a book that explains how to do all of these things in the state of Minnesota. The result of her efforts is

A Will is not enough in Minnesota.

This new book is a continuation of this book. It builds on basic Estate Planning concepts introduced in Chapter 7 of this book and then goes on to introduce other, more sophisticated, Estate Planning methods. Although the topics are sophisticated, the writing style is the same as this book. It is written in plain English. It is intended for use by the average person.

The book is scheduled for release in the fall of 2002. Readers of this book can purchase *A Will is not enough in Minnesota* for $20. This price includes shipping and handling. To check for availability call Eagle Publishing Company at (800) 824-0823.

UPDATE

It is the goal of EAGLE PUBLISHING COMPANY to keep our publications fresh.

As we receive information about changes to the federal or Minnesota law we will post an update to this edition at our Web site:

http://www.eaglepublishing.com